E. B. JAMIESON
ANATOMIST AND SHETLANDER

Love & thanks
from
Norma Jamieson.

E. B. JAMIESON
ANATOMIST AND SHETLANDER

JENNY AND MARTIN EASTWOOD

The Shetland Times Ltd.,
Lerwick.
1999

E. B. Jamieson
Anatomist and Shetlander

ISBN 1 898852 45 6

First published by The Shetland Times Ltd, 1999.

Cover design by The Stafford Partnership, Shetland.

British Library Cataloguing-in-Publication Data
A catalogue record for this book is available from the British Library.

Printed and published by
The Shetland Times Ltd.,
Prince Alfred Street,
Lerwick, Shetland ZE1 0EP, UK.

CONTENTS

LIST OF ILLUSTRATIONS

ACKNOWLEDGEMENTS

THE writing of this account would not have been possible without the anecdotes of former students. The late Dr M. A. (Nick) Caldwell-Nichols of Sharples, Bolton, Lancashire particularly offered support, enthusiasm and his fund of knowledge.

Miss Norna Jamieson, a niece of E. B. Jamieson, was kind enough to let us see personal papers which outlined the history of this remarkable family. The task of writing was greatly aided by access to such accurate information.

John Graham of Lerwick was generous with his time and information he had collected, in particular correspondence from the 1960s with J. P. S. Jamieson who then lived in New Zealand. We are also indebted to the late Edward Thomason for introducing us to valuable sources of information in Shetland.

We owe a great debt to Brian Smith, Shetland Archivist, for his cheerful and kindly help, patiently finding so much background information. We are grateful to the Shetland Archives of the Shetland Islands Council for permission to use archival material. Churchill Livingstone have kindly given permission for the use of the anatomical pictures drawn by E.B.J.

Mrs Jo Currie in the University of Edinburgh Library Special Collections provided valuable information, and thanks are also due to the many other persons who told us so much of E. B. Jamieson and his remarkable family. Anne Jenkinson has had so much to do with the production of this book.

INTRODUCTION

EDWARD Bald Jamieson, who enjoys a singular place in the history of the Edinburgh Medical School, was born in 1876 and died in 1956.

Due to his complex character, his personal remoteness, involvement with students and his powers of scholarship and writing, generations of medical students were affected by his teaching and style. His influence on them was quite remarkable. It is to those who knew him or heard the legends of this man for whom this publication is written as well as to perpetuate his memory.

E. B. J. and Jimmy evoke the memory of E. B. Jamieson and all these names are used in the text depending upon that used by the source of the particular anecdote or recollection.

Whilst researching this book the importance of the context of E. B. Jamieson's life became apparent. He could only be appreciated fully against the background of the folklore, history and education system of Shetland, as well as in the context of his able, successful and mainly academic, family. This book is therefore the story — albeit in brief — of the remarkable Jamieson family.

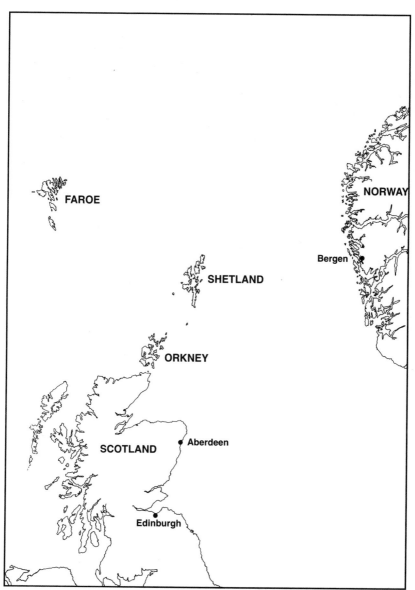

Shetland: "At the crossroads of the North Atlantic."

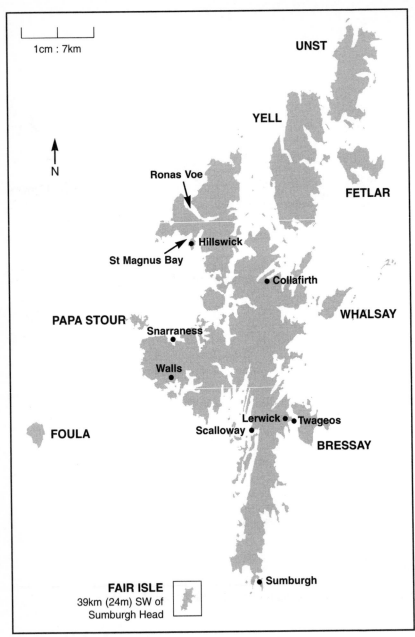

Shetland: Home of the remarkable Jamieson family.

x

PART I

HISTORY

SHETLAND may appear on the same page as the map of Scotland but it is usually in a separate box to indicate that the distance from the mainland is too great to be shown to scale. Indeed it is often said that the nearest railway station to Shetland is in Bergen in Norway. However, it is undeniable Shetland's geographical position "at the crossroads of the North Atlantic" has determined its history.

The first inhabitants of Shetland, the Picts, came from Scotland but exactly where is not certain. It is thought that migrations had been from east to west, hence we may infer that people called Picts were Finnish adventurers from Scandinavia who migrated or were driven westwards about the beginning or shortly before the Christian era. As Shetland is the nearest westwards land from Norway they probably colonised these islands first and in time proceeded westwards by way of Orkney to the mainland of Scotland. There are some place names in which the Finns appear to be commemorated, e.g. Finnistry in Nesting.

The Picts probably occupied the islands for less than a thousand years from c.100AD to c.900AD. Their brochs, burial mounds and standing stones show them to have been a numerous, industrious and intelligent people.

Upwards of 100 brochs and other remains may be traced in Shetland and there are numerous townships called brough. Other derivations are common, such as Burrafirth, Burrastow, Burranesss, Bugarth, Burri Hill, Gossabrough, Brough, Burraland, Burland, Burwick and there are many other names derived from broch such as Sumburgh, Scousburgh and Cunningsburgh.

The Picts were thought to have lived a precarious existence, surviving chiefly from the sheep and cattle pastured on the hills. They perhaps harvested corn which they made into meal by pounding in a stone mortar the, now obsolete, old knocking stane and mill. The Picts depended for their nourishment upon "the harvest of the sea". Their mode of fishing was doubtless of the most primitive kind, particularly rock fishing or "craigs". The extent to which this mode of fishing had been practised in Shetland may be gathered from the vast number of small round holes, known as cupholes, hollowed out by human hands and found all around the islands of Shetland in situations suitable for fishing. The craig fisherman would have found the cuphole very convenient for holding bait and no doubt he utilised it for that purpose. The bait was probably limpets which were prepared not by crushing or bruising into knock-soe, but by being chewed by the fishermen. The craigstane was to the ancient dwellers of the islands what the fishing boat is to the modern fisherman. They supplied him with the means of sustenance when other sources were exhausted. Their ancient markings were probably intended to give the maker some sort of proprietary rights, which would probably descend from father to son.

The Picts lived peacefully among the hills and round the voes of Shetland tending their sheep, cultivating their plots in sheltered nooks, brewing their heather beer and gathering shellfish and birds eggs in season to supplement and add variety to their diet. They constructed earth houses, the remains of which have been found both on hillsides and level fields. The remains are seen as a great mass of stones in a small cuplike hollow where the ground is very deep. Natural caves and helyers along the sea coast were certainly also used as places of shelter by these early inhabitants.

The lives of the Picts were suddenly disturbed by the unwelcome Norsemen, who landed on the coast of the Shetland Islands, plundered, settled and took possession of the territory of the Picts. This colonisation of Shetland from Norway can be dated to the second half of the 9th century and continued for nearly 500 years. Their own country was poor and unable to sustain the Vikings, who therefore invaded and colonised the territory of others. Their religion inspired them with a love for daring exploits, since it was taught that warriors who died in battle were automatically admitted to Valhalla (Heaven). The religion of the Norsemen was largely derived from the constant struggle they had to wage against the savage forces of nature. Hence their Gods, Odin and Thor and the rest forever battled from their home in Asgard against the frost giants and sometimes against the fire giants, both for their own sake and for the sake of the human race who lived in Midgard.

In the Norse culture of that time supreme courage was most highly esteemed but loyalty to ones oath and kindred was also valued. Family feuds could devastate districts and last for generations.

Though quarrelsome the Norsemen had many good qualities. They were hospitable, artistic, fond of athletic sports such as swimming, running, competing in feats of strength or arms and were eager for adventure. They were keen to exercise their wits at such games as chess and the making and solving of riddles and in the construction of complicated verse. They were organisers of great ability.

Once the first Norsemen left, the Picts constructed their brochs or castles as a means of self defence. The sites chosen were such as could best facilitate the transmission of messages by means of signals from one end of the island to the other. The brochs had very low doors, not because the Picts were a dwarfish race but to add to their security. The Picts could easily and instinctively accommodate themselves to the size of their own familiar surroundings, whereas a stranger would be unable to make his way through such small openings with anything like the same speed. Also a narrow passage could be more easily defended than a wide entrance.

A great archaeologist has said that, given the same necessities and limitations, the best modern architect could not construct better buildings than the brochs. And with the same sticks and stones, tiny water courses and absence of tools the best mathematician or engineer could not evolve a better water mill than those erected by the ancient Shetlanders.

The fierce warlike Norsemen came from time to time in great numbers and were more than a match for the Picts who, worn out in their vain struggle and weakened by frequent losses, at last yielded to the conquerors. It is thought that the Picts either left the islands to seek a home elsewhere or were totally annihilated. Tradition favours the latter theory. It is said that a few Picts were spared to teach the art of brewing an intoxicating alcoholic drink from heather, but, rather than divulge their secret, they chose to be killed.

At one time or another, half of Ireland, all of England and a great part of northern Scotland, Normandy, a kingdom in Russia, not to mention Norway, Sweden, Denmark, Iceland and Greenland were ruled by the Norse Vikings whose ruler was known as the Jarl.

The implements used by the early inhabitants of Shetland are from time to time unearthed in a field or moor and their rubbish heaps, consisting chiefly of shells, are frequently found. There are many legends about their burial mounds. Many tall, moss covered standing stones remain but of these rude monuments we are left to ask:

"In what age was't raised?

At whose command?

If Pictish or a Scandinavian hand

Sank deep thy base, and bade thee time withstand?"

Pettasmog is one of the few place names in Shetland which may be regarded as commemorative of the Pictish occupation. The great bulk of Shetland place names are from old Norse. Places do not easily change their names. Though the Scots and then the English languages replaced the old Shetland dialect (Norn), names which had been attached to particular places did not tend to be changed. Hence Scots was pronounced in the old Norse fashion and was liberally sprinkled with Norn words.

From a great number of stone implements found in Shetland it might be supposed that the Stone Age extended over a very long period in these islands. It is probable, however, that even after metal instruments were introduced the primitive stone implements were only very gradually displaced.

The end of Jarldom came in 1468 when the islands were in the possession of Denmark whose king, Christian I, had a daughter Margaret who was to marry James III of Scotland. Her dowry was to be 60,000 florins of which 10,000 were to be paid in cash. Within a year the crown lands and sovereignty in Orkney were pledged for the other 50,000. Only 2000 florins were paid within the year and the crown lands in Shetland were then pledged for the remaining 8000. It was to be a temporary arrangement and the islands were, for that period, to be subject only directly to the King of Scotland or his heir. In 1471 the Scottish Parliament passed an Act which annexed the Earldom of Orkney and the Lordship of Shetland to the Scottish Crown with the provision that they should not be granted in future to anyone except the lawful son or heir of the King.

In 1564 Mary, Queen of Scots, granted the islands to her half brother Lord Robert Stewart in feu for a yearly duty of about 2000 Scots pounds (a feu was perpetual and normally passed to the heirs of the person who received it). Lord Robert was thus in a much stronger legal position than anyone previously. In 1568, before Lord Robert could consolidate his position, Queen Mary conferred the islands on her third husband, James Hepburn, Earl of Bothwell and gave him the title Duke of Orkney. Bothwell, however, had to flee Scotland for Norway where he was arrested and eventually he died in a Danish prison. This allowed Lord Robert Stewart to take back and exceed his original powers and revenues from Orkney and Shetland.

The Reformation carried out in Orkney and Shetland was effective but totally non-violent. It is characteristic of the moderation of the reformation on these islands that there is little evidence of the existence in that period of the Presbyterian idea that authority should be in the hands, not of bishops or commissioners, but of committees of ministers called presbyteries. A presbytery does not seem to have operated effectively in Shetland at any time before 1638 when the episcopal system was for a time abolished. Lord Robert did not, in his early years, have many dealings in person with Shetland and in 1571 Robert delegated his powers as Foud of Shetland to his half brother Laurence Bruce Cultmalindie. Bruce abused his authority in every possible way according to the elaborate complaints against him drawn up by the inhabitants of Shetland. In 1577 he tampered with the official weights and measures so that he could collect more butter and cloth than was really due to him. He imposed a tax on pigs which led people to avoid pig keeping. He exacted compulsory service in the provision of boats for transport among the islands and he billeted his followers on the Shetlanders. He built Muness Castle as his residence. Earl Patrick, who succeeded Earl Robert in 1591, seems to have more direct dealings with Shetland. Before 1592 he built the house at Sumburgh, the ruins of which were named Yarlshof by Sir Water Scott. About 1600 Patrick built a castle at Scalloway and at least once he toured the islands personally to hold local courts. Some of the earlier reported oppressions appear no longer to have operated in Patrick's time.

The period of Patrick Stewart's rule was the last phase under the old order of Shetland before the islands were assimilated in law and institutions into the rest of the Scottish Kingdom. There is no evidence that the agreement by which the sovereignty of the islands was pledged to Scotland in 1469 included a provision that the Norse law should be preserved. It was however preserved and the Scottish Parliament more than once acknowledged that the legal system in

Orkney and Shetland was different from the rest of Scotland. There was still a local court or "ting" in each district, a local "Foud" who gave his decision in disputes between neighbours, a "Law Rightman" who was responsible for weights and measures and the inspection of dykes and ranselmen for the detection of theft. The Earl does not appear to have appointed his own dependents as local officers or to the local courts as Laurence Bruce had done, though he did use the whole system for his own advantage. According to the law, the most common punishment was a fine. The courts constantly imposed fines for trivial breaches of the many traditional regulations as well as for old, half forgotten offences and this all enriched the Earl and impoverished the natives, sometimes to such an extent that they had to part with their land.

It was after Earl Patrick's fall that the Norse Law was abolished. James Law, who had been appointed Bishop of Orkney in 1606, informed King James VI in 1608 about the Earl's practices. Patrick was imprisoned in Edinburgh in 1609 and was executed in 1615, after one of his sons had raised a rebellion in Orkney. Bishop Law himself then attained great power and was almost as ambitious and self seeking as the Earl had been, for like the Earl he was Sheriff and Justiciar. The bishop did not however own the Earldom estates which were again vested in the Crown and his position was not hereditary. The King was at this time energetically engaged in extending and strengthening his authority and it was part of his policy to make use of bishops, rather than hereditary nobles in maintaining order through the country.

The Earldom lands were mainly in the family of the Earls of Morton from 1543 to 1766 when they were sold to Sir Laurence Dundas.

The dispossession of Earl Patrick and the abolition of the Norse Law put an end to the possibility that developments in Orkney and Shetland would be similar to those in the Channel Islands and the Isle of Man which still retain so many of their own institutions. From 1611, the Earldom of Orkney and Lordship of Shetland ceased to have a separate political history, although the islands continued to have their own distinctive social and economic history. They did remain something of a land apart, if only because communications were poor.

Within Shetland there were no roads and transport was mainly by sea. There was no regular transport service between Shetland and Scotland until well after 1800. Communication was actually more frequent with the continent than with Scotland. The connection with Norway remained close but there were more important economic ties with Germany and with Holland. Merchants, who were often called "Dutch" were really "Deutsch" or German. They were mostly from Hamburg and Bremen and were responsible for much of Shetland's trade in the 16th and 17th century. The merchants traded food, clothing, boating and fishing equipment and luxury articles in return for fish, butter and oil. Foreign money was currency in the islands and the German language was quite well known. The real Dutchmen, or Hollanders as they were called, were concerned with the herring fishing.

Big changes took place after 1700. The Dutch fishing fleet never recovered from the blow it received in 1703 when the French destroyed their herring fleet. It was not until well through the 19th century that natives of Shetland began to play a significant part in the herring fishing. The operation of German merchants was adversely affected in 1712 by a tax on foreign salt and a bounty on fish cured with British salt by British merchants.

In the early 18th century the Shetland tenants were too much at the mercy of the lairds. Almost the only escape, apart from naval service into which men were often conscripted by press gangs, was the whale fishing off Greenland and the Davis Straits. This fishing was conducted by English and Scots who recruited many Shetlanders at Lerwick for their crews. The Shetlanders were in great demand as seamen but even more as boatmen and harpooners and the chance of adventure combined with relatively high wages attracted many young men from every district.

In the 18th century a new phase in Shetland life began. The lairds themselves took on the function of merchants. They now possessed most of the lands of Shetland and the great majority of the people were at once tenants and employees of these merchant landlords. The landlords were the purchasers of fish, cattle, wool and hosiery and were also the salesmen from whom, alone, the people could buy such commodities as they could not produce themselves. The Shetlanders had no security of tenure or protection against the raising of their rents. They were almost perpetually in debt to their masters, who could dictate both rents and prices.

Press gangs also grievously harassed the isles and it is difficult to give an adequate picture of them. The pressed Shetlander was worse off than a convict. The convicts would at least be set free alive, whereas death by battle, wounds or disease took a 50 per cent toll of all the island's press ganged seamen. A convict's family would, if necessary, have been maintained by the state while the seaman's family was usually left, sometimes for years without even knowledge of the fate of its breadwinner.

The Shetlanders were almost entirely self supporting though the harvest of the land supplemented by the produce of the sea was their sole means of subsistence. Even today one may hear the old speaking of the "scarce years". Stories have been handed down of the seasons of want and the extremes to which people were sometimes reduced. Near the sites of old townships enormous quantities of shells, particularly whelks, may be dug up showing that these had been extensively used for food. Supplies were drawn from the crops of oats, bere, potatoes and cabbage and from the prevalent and available sheep and fish. These commodities, through trade, still form the staple means of support.

In a Shetland croft of the 18th century, the dwellinghouse, barn and byre were built together so that access could be had to all parts from within. The only entrance to the dwelling was commonly through the byre. In a corner of the barn, there was a kiln for drying corn, which was about six feet long by three feet broad. On the wall hung a straw mat on which the corn was winnowed. In the barn also was the handmill used for grinding the corn. In the corner of the room the knocking stane was used to shell bere or barley, used as a delicacy for holy days and Sunday dinners.

Tea was almost unknown, blaandi-kaulik (sour whey) and swats (the liquid in which oatmeal has been steeped) were used instead. Fish was the chief article of food and almost every house had a skeo (open built hut for drying fish) in which fresh fish was stored for future use. Fish for home consumption was salted and sold but was also preserved in various other ways such as being reested (smoke dried), blawn (dried in the wind) or gizzened (dried in the sun).

The liver of the fresh fish was extensively used and was the chief ingredient of numerous nutritious dishes. To fish liver may be attributed the hardiness of the old Shetlander and the almost perfect immunity from the fatal forms of some diseases.

In the crofter's home no person was idle. The grown up females of the household prepared wool for the loom which could be made into underclothing for the family or dyed with blue-litt (indigo-dye), old man's skrottie (a lichen), or yellowin' girse (grass), for suiting, for the master of the house, or dresses for the females.

The common pastimes when neighbours came in, particularly at Hallowmas celebrations, were various versions of "going to wads" (forfeits) and "layin' up guddicks", that is telling riddles. For example

"roond like a mill stane,

lugget like a cat,

standin' upo' three legs - can you guess dat"

Answer - a kettle.

Or "four fingers and four gangers

twa luckers and twa crookers

twa laavers and ae dildillie-daunder"

Answer - a cow.

Straw was put to numerous uses by the old Shetlander. It was food and bedding for his cattle, it thatched his roof and formed his couch at night. The very seat on which he sat was made of straw. It furnished another favourite subject for evening amusement. The first person of the party commenced by asking the next "what ös is strae", each person then had to answer for what is straw useful and then ask the question of the next person and so on round and round until someone at last failed to find a use for straw that had not been previously mentioned. The loser then paid a forfeit.

When Hallowmas was past the winter duties began. Each woman carded and spun wool and made cloth for her own wear. The social disposition of the people led them to spend much of their time, especially in the long winter evenings, in each other's houses telling stories of the sea, tales of adventure, trows and witches, stories of smugglers' wrecks together with talk of more practical affairs both general and domestic.

Winter was the chief season of festivity. As a rule, all marriages took place during the three winter months.

The 20th December was Tammasmass E'en and the day following is Tammasmass day in which no manner of work could be done,

"ta shap or shu, ta bake or brew,

ta reel a pirm or wind a clew,

lo Strupalty will tak you."

Christmas Day was a day of plenty, when everybody old or young wore something new. The round peat fire blazed, the house was well lit with an irregular tallow dip. The day was spent in feasting. At night, the service of the local fiddler was called for and the merry go round of the Shetland Rant was kept up from house to house until four and twenty day (18th January) when the exhausted larders reminded the people that it was time to resume the more stern duties of life.

The Shetland house was traditionally heated by burning peat. Peats are best used in the year after cutting. In March before the peats were cut, the ground was "flae-ed", meaning that the turves were cut off the area prior to casting. In May the peats were first cut using a tool known as a tushker. They were then built into a honeycomb dyke to facilitate drying and left to lie flat for two weeks, then raised and made into a wigwam and left for a further two or three weeks. If they were not then dry enough, they were turned and a wigwam of about six peats was built, which was left for another three weeks. In July, before the rain, the peats were bagged in sacks or a basket known as a kishie, and taken home for use the following year.

The earliest years of the 19th century were to Shetland a time of hunger, fear and general wretchedness and a seemingly endless bitter struggle for survival. The islands did not produce sufficient food for more than five months of the year and most people lived mainly and monotonously on fish and potatoes.

The importance of an item in a culture is indicated by the number of different words in the language describing it. For example in Inuit there are many words to describe snow and desert people describe sand in many ways. In Shetland during the nineteenth century, hunger was variously described.

"Clung as a peat" meaning hungry.

"A hungry man is an angry man."

"Hungry dogs never bark weel."

"Hungry bairns greet sair."

"It's a braw wife that can bring but what's no ben."

"The thing can sair dee and me that canna' sair twatree."

"Better a cauld bite than nae bread."

"Better a moose i' da kale than nae kitchen".

Associated with poverty and hunger was need. Lending and helping were therefore well described.

"They that gie me a little wid see me living."

"Borrow and lend helps mony a man."

"Gifgaf maks guid friends."

"The weel-willed man is da beggar's bridder."

The crofter had a constant struggle to earn money for the rent which was comparatively high, while the price obtainable for his livestock and wool was extremely low. At this time the principal and almost the only export of the isles was salt fish.

The Reform Bill of 1832 gave Shetland, for the first time, a voice in the management of her own affairs. She had at last a share with Orkney in returning a representative to Parliament.

Young people were certainly not pampered in the nineteenth century. Neither were adults. Laws harsh in themselves were harshly administered. Offences against property were especially liable to severe punishment as in the example five men charged with stealing some rabbit traps who were sentenced to 20 days hard labour each. The church too in dealing with its members exercised a severity which today seems strange: "November 24th, 1862 - The Free Church of Unst found it necessary to suspend 20 of their members for dancing and two for travelling in a vessel that sailed on a Sunday."

On 16th July, 1832, there was a major disaster at sea involving many districts, especially the North Isles and the east coast of Shetland. Several hundred boats had put to sea in fine weather and were out at the far fishing grounds 30 to 40 miles from land when a hurricane burst upon them with such violence that in the islands, where savage gales were not uncommon even in summer, that day was remembered for more than 100 years as "the bad day". Never again would a sixern's crew willingly put out to sea on that date in July. The dreadful storm raged almost unabated for four days. At the end of 24 hours of suspense 60 boats and 300 men were missing. In the week that followed some were found but 105 men had perished.

In March 1837 a Reverend James Everett Newcastle wrote "I find it difficult give you anything like a description of the deplorable state of things in these islands. A number of persons have within the last two months left our shores.

Every vessel has taken less or more and some of them have been crowded with men, women and children flying from starvation, some emigrating to America, others to places of which they knew nothing."

In the 1840s Government employment was found on land for some men in the making of roads. Altogether about 100 miles of roads were constructed. They were the so-called "meal roads", the labourers receiving, in meal, the equivalent of about three old pence (1.5p) per day.

In the report from the Synod of Lerwick in 1837 we learn that "In 1835 the crops of Shetland were deficient, the ling fishing failed, the herring fishing along the whole east coast of Scotland was unproductive, the whale fishing was worse than unproductive and during the succeeding winter an unprecedented mortality among sheep, horses and cattle swept off nearly the whole of their stocks." In 1836 the ling fishing was again unproductive, the herring and whale fishing were total failures and thus all who engaged in those pursuits, i.e. nearly the whole male population of the islands, were involved in still greater difficulties. Under these famine conditions appeals were made to the South for charity meal to keep the people alive.

The 1840s saw further decline in fishing while on land the potato crops failed for some years in succession until in 1846 with the total failure of that crop and the high price of corn the islanders found themselves on the brink of starvation.

This is the background from which large numbers of Shetlanders emigrated. Some sought freedom from the poverty of the islands, others, like the Jamiesons were drawn away by their thirst for education.

FOLKLORE

THE distinction between Shetland history and Shetland folklore is sometimes difficult to define. In the late 19th century, as today, there was a feeling that standards were deteriorating. In John Spence's *Shetland Folklore* (1899) one reads: "There is undoubtedly a growing tendency among the younger people of the present day to undervalue or neglect what has come down to us from former times. To understand the charm of the folklore one must picture for oneself the old grandfather or grandmother telling to the eager bairns around the blazing peat fire on the long winter evenings, tales of trows and witches, spirits and apparitions, until at last the children who had gathered from neighbouring houses felt afraid to venture back alone. In those days, traditional tales were the form in which, information was conveyed by tale and story, and not by books as now. To save the relics of the past and interest the rising generation in them one must use the printed page. The young folk do not listen now; they read". Now the pendulum has swung fully and the late 20th century complaint is that children are attracted away from reading by the spoken word of radio, television and video.

It is worthy of note that there were and still remain numerous legends in Shetland which may be regarded as of Finnish origin or at least associated in the minds of old Shetlanders with real or imaginary beings whom they called Fittens. These were persons supposed to be descendants of Finns who were accredited with extraordinary powers. They could render themselves visible or invisible at will. They could metamorphose themselves into beasts, birds or fish. It is even said that they could assume the appearance of a beetle. Hence we have to this day the witchy clock and the turtiel, two kinds of beetles. They were supposed to understand the language of the corbies, (ravens) and this often proved to be of considerable advantage as in the following tale.

An old man possessed of this Finnish art had lost a young horse. He wandered up hill and down dale for several days without finding the stray animal. One morning two corbies alighted on the knoll near his house and talked to each other. From this the man, interpreting the corbies speech, found that his own horse had fallen over a bank.

The Finns were said to be the only being who could safely ride the Nyuggel. The Nyuggel, or Nicker, was a water deity that appeared in the form of a sleek horse, having erect mane and tail like the "rim, o' a muckle wheel". He was found by the banks of burns and the margins of lonely lakes playing his tricks on water mills where the owner had neglected to give him an offering. If any nocturnal wanderer, mistaking a Nyuggel for a real horse, mounted the beast he was instantly carried into the middle of the nearest lake or dam and left there struggling in the water while the creature rushed towards the opposite shore. It is not said that anyone was actually drowned by a Nyuggel but only the Finns could ride the water horse.

A few legends of the fabled race of giants have come down to us. These stories are usually connected with the standing stones, or remarkable rocks or boulders:

A story is told of two giants called Herman and Sax who once lived in Unst. The former resided in a large cave in the neighbourhood of Hermanness, called Herman's Ha', while Sax occupied a subterranean cavern in the side of the Muckle Poby called Sax's Ha'. Now it happened that Herman had caught a whale at Burghfirth and as it was exceptionally large he asked his neighbour Sax for a loan of his kettle, a great cauldron set in a cavity in the rocks, in which to boil his gigantic prey. But Sax having an eye to business would only lend the kettle on condition that he got half the whale. These terms seemed exorbitant to Herman and, indignant at the churlish conduct of his neighbour, he seized a huge boulder and hurled it at Sax. He overshot the mark and the stone fell into the sea near the

Horns of Hagmark where it sands high above the waves and bears the name of Herman's Stack.

Trows or hill folk were supposed to have had the same passions as mortals. They married and were given in marriage. They indulged their appetites of the good things of this life. They even required the services of the children of men for fiddlers, howdies (mid-wives) and nurses and at the end of the 19th century there were people alive whose forebears were said to have been so employed.

A standing stone once stood near the old churchyard of Northwick in Unst which also concerned the giant Sax. This stone had a hole in it and its origin was traditionally said to be that the giant Sax had come to Kirkatoon, where a famous howdie lived, and whose services were required at Sax's house. Not finding a suitable fastening for the horse he was riding, he drove the monolith into the ground, and pushed his thumb through it, making a hole into which he tied his horse's rein.

Women at the time of childbearing were especially liable to be taken by the hill folk and hence the midwife was generally an expert in the art of preserving her charge from the trow. When a birth was about to take place it was customary to borrow a black cock and bring it into the house. The black cock detected any unseen presence and announced the same by crowing at every hour. Thus when a cock was heard crowing at an unseasonable time it was understood that some person doomed to die (fey) was within hearing. If a person had met with any serious fright the living heart was torn from the breast of the cock and applied bleeding to the left breast of the individual affected.

The trows sometimes rendered themselves visible to ordinary mortals and are said to have left behind them some of their own domestic utensils, the possession of which was believed to be very lucky.

As recently as 1899 some persons were marked as being particularly lucky and those who were supposed to be skilled in the black art were spoken of as Norway Finns. A person skilled in the black art deprived his or her neighbours of the profit of their milk and butter. Every housewife tried to keep her own and used as much as possible to avoid such loss. Persons intent on bewitching a neighbour endeavoured to obtain the loan of some domestic utensil, especially about the time when a cow was expected to calf. But a wise woman would lend nothing at such a time. If a suspected person called and even asked for a drink of blaand (sour whey) the goodwife would seize a live coal and chase the unwanted visitor out of the door, throwing the fire after her, while she exclaimed "twee-tee-see-dee to ill-vaumed trooker!"

There were certain seasons when witchcraft was most dreaded. The youngsters searched for four leafed clovers (smora), the finding of which was considered extremely lucky. Anyone possessing this holy plant was believed to be protected against the evils of the witches.

Of all Shetlanders, the fisherman appear to have been the most superstitious. No doubt this arose largely from the nature of their hazardous and precarious job. When a fisherman left his house to go to his boat, it was considered most unlucky to call after him, even if he had left something essential behind. He was most meticulous about who he met on the way to the boat in case they should have the evil eye or an "ill-fit". It was, perhaps surprisingly, considered a good omen to meet an imbecile or a person deformed from birth. These were called "Gude's pör". After meeting one of such, if the voyage had been at all prosperous the individual was rewarded with an aamos (gift). A person who attempted to cross a fisherman's path while on his way to the boat intended to do him faat (harm). When harm was really done, the fisherman coming to the point of crossing, took out his tully (sea knife) and made a scratch in the form of a cross, saying, after spitting, the words "Twee-tee-see-dee". The sign of the Cross was considered an antedote to the intended evil and spitting was an emphatic expression of contempt for the illwisher.

The Shetland fisherman had quite a vocabulary of old Norse words which were generally used at sea, particularly in speaking of land objects. It was deemed most unlucky not to use these expressions. No doubt the belief lingered that the ancient gods of the Norsemen still exercised power over the ocean. Hence it was considered prudent to use at least such words as had reference to the old faith. The old fishermen never spoke of things being lost or broken and they never mentioned the end of anything. To be lost was expressed as having "gone to itself"; broken, "made up".

The various articles of furniture about a fisherman's house in the olden days were made from driftwood (raaga trees) and the cracking sounds occasionally heard from such articles were said to indicate a change in the weather. It was also believed that certain days of the week related to the weather. For example, a change for the better on Sunday was considered a favourable omen, but a bright Monday foretold a dark week. Wednesday's weather was true and Friday was supposed to be either the best or the worst day of the week.

The success or failure of the fishing largely determined the prosperity or otherwise of the Shetlanders. Not surprisingly there were many old adages about how the weather might be determined for example by the movements and conduct of certain birds and animals. To hear crows crying after sunset indicated that the next day would be fair; the flight inland of the rain goose (the red throated diver) was particularly significant. The weather was then likely to be favourable, but when its flight was directed towards the sea the opposite was expected. Hence:

"Whin da raingös gengs ta da sea, pit your boat anunder da lee;

Whin da raingös flees ta da hill, tak your boat and geng whaar you will."

Cocks crowing or hens out and about while rain was falling was a sign that it would soon be fair. A cat sitting with her back to the fire indicated snow may be coming, whilst the cat washing her face with both forepaws was a sure sign of coming rain. When the cat was observed to be sleeping with her head turned up, fair weather might be expected, but "whin da cat sleeps on her harn (brains), its coming wind".

There were a host of occurrences which were seen as bad omens at a wedding. Anyone carrying a burden and crossing the path of the bridal party, a bird flying from right to left over the newly wedded pair, a boat seen to be leaving land during the march to church, a raven croaking within hearing or a child crying as the couple passed would all have been omens of bad luck. If none of these bad omens occurred then the young pair could expect to be happy all of their lives.

The object of Hallowmas sports was to get an idea about the future. This was attempted by the activities of "drappin glasses", and "siftin siller". "Drappin glasses" was performed by dropping a small portion of the white of an egg into a glass of water. The shape of the fall indicated the future in matters of love, fortune and death. In "siftin siller" the operator went into an empty room which contained a mirror opposite the window. He took his position with his back to the window and facing the mirror. Then with three silver coins in a sieve he sifted away steadfastly gazing at the mirror in which he observed the view reflected through the window. While this was going on he expected to behold passing before his astonished gaze in a sort of panoramic order the whole of his future life.

In the festivities of the olden times there seemed to be special respect paid to the number three. For example, when births, marriages or deaths occurred there were three feasts in connection with each. There was the blyde feast when the child was born, the fittin feast when the mother got up and resumed her duties and the christening when the child was baptised. In connection with a marriage there was the spörin, the contract, and the bridal which commonly lasted three days. Spör means to ask or enquire, that is the occasion when the bridegroom formally asked the consent of the brides parents. Even at the final and most solemn event of life, three feasts were again observed, first the kistin, (the placing of the body in the coffin), then the funeral and lastly the condolences.

EDUCATION

THE only schools which existed prior to the 18th century were "adventure" schools. These were private schools conducted in cottages, usually run by elderly women. The education was paid for in kind, for example milk, peat, or fish. An old woman in Bixter held a school in her house where the children did sums in "ess" which was the ash from the hearth. There was another similar school in Lerwick. For reading, the Bible was passed from hand to hand. If the child faltered the teacher, also being unable to read it, might say that the word was in Latin.

"Instruction in letters" at this time was mainly given to the people by "decayed" gentlewomen, usually sisters or daughters of merchants or ministers. There is no record of ladies of the landed class, however "decayed", ever condescending to teach. In every parish there were two or three such teachers who often combined teaching with other occupations. If the teacher had a home of her own, the children were taught there, otherwise the neighbours would combine and build a "cot" for a schoolroom to which each child brought a stool to sit on and a daily peat for the fire, while the teacher slept in the house of each parent in turn, one night for each pupil.

The gentry were educated by tutors and governesses. Winter was the time devoted to learning. Each laird had a town house to which the family went for the winter and it was fairly easy for one tutor or governess to teach the children of several families. In one notable respect Shetland gentry differed from those in the south where tutors and governesses were kept in very subordinate positions. Shetland was a happy hunting ground for tutors and governesses who often married into the family of their employers. Parish ministers of the period were usually tutors or schoolmasters prior to their induction.

Scotland established a national system of education long before England. But behind the Highland Line conditions of squalor and ignorance existed which horrified the progressive lowland Scots and touched their consciences. In 1707 the Assembly of the Church of Scotland appealed for help to found a Society to Propagate Christian Knowledge in the Highlands and Islands. A patent incorporating the Society was obtained in 1709. From the first its affairs were managed centrally and with great care and economy. Collections were received from the churches and a Royal Bounty assisted the cause. The schools were supplementary to the parish schools, being placed in remote places, and were not intended to relieve the parishes of their obligations. Charity schools or "society schools" were those which were established by the SSPCK (Society in Scotland for Promoting Christian Knowledge).

The first Shetland SSPCK school opened in Walls in 1713. The teacher was supposed to move from one school to another at the end of a given period, usually 12 months. They were thus sometimes also termed "ambulatory schools".

Under hereditary legislation there was an Act of Parliament empowering heritors to erect and maintain schools in each parish. The parish authorities could enforce the upkeep of the schools. The statute determined that the cost of these schools would be borne 50 per cent by the landowners with the levy being proportional to their acreage and 50 per cent by the people of the community.

The schools were known as "heritor schools", "legal schools" and later as "parochial schools".

Sometimes the landlords would pay their share but then charge an increased rent, usually in kind, from their tenants. Sometimes landlords said that they did not want to spend money on a school which would not benefit all of their tenants. The provision of authority, even by Acts of Parliament, is of no value when there is no one to insist on enforcement.

Shetland, unlike Orkney, had no high school nor any fixed school until 1724. In that year the Heritors of Shetland held a great meeting in Scalloway to discuss ways and means for establishing "legal" parish schools. Also in 1741 the presbytery granted a petition for salaries for three ambulatory schools in the islands. Of these the grant to Sandness was given for two years only, as "other parishes have also need of education". The session returned hearty thanks to the presbytery on behalf of the Sandness parishioners who at once set about building a school. There had been so much trouble about former schools, the laird claiming them and putting tenants into them whenever they fell vacant that the people wondered how to prevent that happening again. They built the school in the corner of the ancient churchyard of St Ninian where the laird had no jurisdiction and the building stood for over 70 years.

In the eighteenth century many teachers had some disability or deformity which prevented them from following the able-bodied local men into the fishing industry. The first appointee to the Sandness school was a James Cheyne, session clerk, who took office on the 27th October, 1741, after examination by the presbytery.

In 1742 the proposal was made to move him to another parish but this was vigorously opposed and James Cheyne continued in Sandness. However, the presbytery refused to fix the school and up until 1748 James Cheyne was annually instructed to move to another parish where the presbytery saw a great need for Christian instruction. The people of that parish, however, did not think it worthwhile to accept him and refused to erect a school. It was not until 1758 that the society consented to fix the schools. James Cheyne died in 1755 and his son, George Cheyne, succeeded him and continued teaching until 1792.

The presbyterial examinations of society schools are recorded and it is interesting to note the subjects and tests of the examinations and the format of the visits.

The examiners met, opened with prayer and read over the society's rules, and the instructions to visitors and correspondents of schools. Then, "having purged their minds of all malice and prejudice, they proceeded to the school where the master and quaking children awaited them, with assembled parents of the district. They first examined the state of the building. Then they enquired of the Master whether the parents were amenable to their duties of sending forth children, fulfilling their school dues, upkeep of service and fees, and providing books and peats for the pupils, and the parents were commended or reprimanded according to their desserts".

Next there was an enquiry into the state of the books used by the children, those whose books showed evidence of carelessness were rebuked. The lists of scholars was checked. These gave the name, age and parentage of each pupil, attainments on entering school, present stage of progress and attendance. A very careful note was made of progress and the table of reports show that much individual attention was given to each child, for no two of them were reading at the same part of their books. These tables also showed that most of the pupils could read when the society schools first opened, for only the very young children began at ABC in the first society report.

There was a great deal of committing to memory. The teaching of writing was terribly hampered by the lack of paper, showing that slates had not yet come into use. The arrival of half a ream of paper and a box of books was especially noted.

For writing the parents had to produce quills. The bigger boys could make and mend pens but usually only the master had a knife and his time during the writing lessons was largely taken up mending and pointing pens. We are apt to forget the origin of the pen knife. Ink was also hard to obtain and it was sometimes made of milk and grime from the cooking pans. There is a recipe for making ink preserved in the register. There were also problems in relation to arithmetic. Eventually some genius proposed to print the arithmetical tables on the covers of catechisms, to help in the teaching of the principles of arithmetic. The Assembly, after much hesitation, over this blending of sacred and secular matters, implemented the suggestion and all the catechisms thereafter are so printed.

Attendance was marked as constant, frequent, often, now and then, seldom and very seldom. Some of the parents reported that their big boys would not go to school. In such cases the master was empowered to send out as many of the pupils as could bring him in by force and on his arrival to punish him by thrashing him on the breeches with the tawse. The lack of clothes and shoes was never offered as a cause of non-attendance.

There were also a number of emphases in the long reports prepared for the society, drawing attention to the disadvantages under which progress was made. Later reports show that reading, writing and arithmetic, committing to memory and church music are all conscientiously taught and appreciated. The copies of reports ceased after 1758.

The society commissioned the Reverend John Kemp as the first Inspector of Schools in 1789. He reported in 1799 to the SSPCK that there were only two parochial schools in Shetland. The society then intimated that it would withdraw all grants from parishes which did not erect parochial (legal) schools. This threat was so effective that by 1820 there were nine parochial schools in Shetland and grammar, geography, book keeping and navigation were all on the curriculum. The society supported the teaching of girls and gave special grants for the teaching of sewing and other hand crafts to balance instruction in navigation.

A key person in the development of education in the Shetland Islands was Reverend James Buchan, Minister of Walls and Sandness, who succeeded in obtaining the establishment of three schools in Walls (1713), Sandness and Papa Stour. In 1829 the last school was established in North Yell. The SSPCK was no longer required to provide schools when the national system of education was fully developed, and this provision was withdrawn after 1880.

In the early nineteenth century schooling was, in the main, very primitive and elementary and stopped at an early age. Children had to share in the work of the croft and also health conditions were poor. Most children were flea bitten and lousy. Scabies was common and the children often had festering sores (impetigo). Tuberculosis was prevalent and smallpox sometimes occurred. On account of almost complete absence of sanitation typhoid and typhus occurred frequently.

Formal education had previously played a very small part in the life of the Shetland community and the standard had varied greatly from district to district. The teacher's salary, as much as £30 in some districts, was augmented by the fees charged. The charges were usually 1s per term each for reading, writing and arithmetic. There were two terms in the year; the three months before and three months after New Year's Day. Secondary education was only available privately until November 1862, the date of the opening of the Anderson Institute.

1872 was a very important milestone in Shetland history. The Scottish Education Act made education compulsory for all children between seven and 14 years, unless they resided more than three miles from the nearest school. These changes were very drastic indeed. Hitherto, few children had more than three terms at school, and even if they had attended for four terms, it amounted to a total of one year at most. Now practically all children when they reached the age of seven had to go to school and continue for seven years and attend each year for more than 40 weeks. Eager as parents were to give their children some education, this was a shock and the attendance officer had, at first, the difficult task in bringing reluctant scholars to school. New and larger schools had to be built, many of them on new sites, in order to bring as many children as possible within the prescribed distance from a school. The work took some time and most of the present schools date from 1873 to 1880.

The peoples, appreciation of education did not end solely in seeking it for their own children. They also contributed willingly to collections for promoting knowledge elsewhere. Four collections may be noted, especially one for a college in Jersey, one for a bridge in Kelso, one for a school in Breslaw and one for converting Red Indians to Christianity. In the same conditions better work could not be done than that accomplished by the pioneers of formal education in Shetland. This was the context into which Robert Jamieson was born. He was a person to whom learning was pleasure, both personally and in promoting excellence in the education of his family and pupils.

1. Snarraness, West Burrafirth, c.1991.   *Photo by J. W. Jamieson*

2. The road to Snarraness today.

NEW SCHOOL-HOUSE AND SCHOOL, SANDNESS, SHETLAND.

SANDNESS, SHETLAND, 10th January 1871.

SIR,

The above woodcut gives a view of the Schoolhouse and School which, through the liberality of Clergymen, Schoolmasters, and other friends of education in the South, I have succeeded in erecting in this locality.

It is a plain, neat, and substantial building, well lighted and ventilated, erected on a piece of ground granted by the landlord to the School for ever, and will, I hope, prove a blessing to the poor people of the district for generations to come.

The district benefited by the School is situated on the north - west of the Mainland of Shetland, contains a population of 606, is distant 10 miles from the Parochial School, and the School attendance has of late years increased from 30 to 70 Scholars.

The old School buildings, which were built in 1790, and were at best of an inferior description, had fallen into such a ruinous condition as to become uninhabitable, and they either had to be rebuilt or the salary would be withdrawn.

The general poverty of the people was such that they could do nothing, and I could not think of their losing their School without my doing everything in my power to help them. It has been a hard struggle, has occupied every spare moment of my time for upwards of two years; and had the appeals on behalf of the sick and wounded soldiers not seriously interfered with my scheme, I believe I would have succeeded in raising funds to complete my buildings in a satisfactory manner; but I am sorry to say that I am still £35 short of the sum necessary to finish the Schoolroom.

The School is open to all, and is attended by the children of every denomination in the district ; and as I have no sympathy with the advocates of a secular system of education, I have done my utmost to secure that the Bible shall always be taught in the School.

I am sorry to trouble you, but I am anxious to finish my Schoolroom so as to enable my Scholars to pursue their studies in comfort ; and if you will be kind enough to favour me with a small subscription, or bring my case under the notice of any lady or gentleman whom you think might sympathise with me, you will exceedingly oblige,

SIR,

Your obedient Servant,

ROBERT JAMIESON.

Address.—ROBERT JAMIESON,
SCHOOLMASTER, SANDNESS, SHETLAND.

THE MANSE, WALLS, SHETLAND, 1st October 1870.

I CERTIFY that MR ROBERT JAMIESON, Schoolmaster at Sandness in this Parish, who is making laudable efforts to complete the erection of a suitable Schoolhouse and School in that district, has my entire sympathy in the object he has in view. The property on which the School stands is much burdened, and the proprietor therefore able to do little more than grant a site, with a small patch of ground. The people are almost entirely fishermen and small crofters, and can give no effectual aid. They are very desirous, however, to give their children a good education—have great respect for, and like their teacher well, who, in a numerous and well-conducted School, is doing a great deal of good in the district.

ARCHIBALD NICHOL,
Minister of the Parish of Walls and Sandness.

3. Woodcut of the schoolhouse, Sandness, Shetland, c.1871, letter from Robert Jamieson requesting financial support for the completion of his school, and Archibald Nichol's supporting letter.   *Courtesy of Shetland Archives*

4. Robert Jamieson, schoolteacher, Sandness (1858-99).

Courtesy of John J. Graham

5. Christina Jamieson before she emigrated to New Zealand.

6. Christina Jamieson (in Shetland cardigan) and others in the garden of Twageos.

© *Shetland Museum*

7. Twageos House.

8. Christina and E. B. Jamieson at Twageos.

9. E. B. Jamieson lecturing in the anatomy theatre.

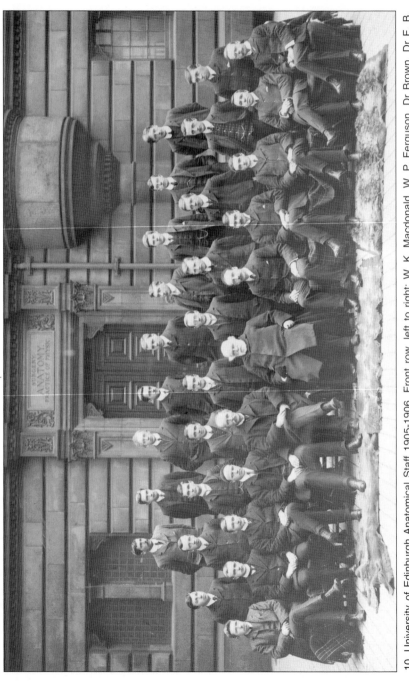

10. University of Edinburgh Anatomical Staff 1905-1906. Front row, left to right: W. K. Macdonald, W. P. Ferguson, Dr Brown, Dr E. B. Jamieson, Professor Cunningham, Sir William Turner (Principal) Dr Waterston, Dr Turton Price, David Robertson, A. L. Thornley, C. E. A. Coldicutt.

PART II
THE JAMIESON FAMILY

ROBERT JAMIESON

ROBERT Jamieson, E. B. Jamieson's father, was born at Sandness on the 19th April, 1827. His parents were crofters. Robert's education was in a little school at Cruisdale, taught by a William Pole. In those days education in a small country school was elementary, only the basic subjects, reading, writing and arithmetic were taught. Attendance was dependent upon the requirements of the crofts, particularly in the better weather when children were needed for croft work.

During his early infancy Robert had an illness, probably poliomyelitis, as a result of which he had a weakness of his left leg, and required crutches for walking. All able-bodied men of his time became fishermen or crofters but Robert, unlike his four brothers, could not go to sea because of his lameness. Robert Jamieson began as a boy to learn shoe-making though even at this time his great intellect was evident. He always expressed his wish to be a school teacher and although he was left an orphan at the age of ten he worked towards that goal. At 14, despite being self-taught, he was recommended as a tutor to the family of Thomas Adie of Voe. Although he was now self-supporting this did not satisfy his perfectionist nature. He wanted to obtain certification as a teacher. At the age of 17 he used the money that he had earned from tutoring to travel to Edinburgh for a course of training at the Church of Scotland Training College.

On completing this course in 1848, aged 21, he was appointed to take charge of Brugarth School, Whiteness which was run by the SSPCK (Society in Scotland for the Propagation of Christian Knowledge). The salary was between £15 and £20 a year. He worked successfully and happily in Whiteness for ten years, making lifelong friendships and earning the respect of the people of the district.

He continued his quest for education throughout his life, becoming widely read in literature, politics, Scandinavian Law and the history and traditions of Shetland. He was familiar with the genealogy of every Shetland family of note and knowledgeable about local habits, tales and traditions. At his death he left an unfinished history of Shetland.

Although Robert Jamieson claimed to be a Conservative, he had, atypically for a Conservative of his time, very liberal ideas. He was an Elder and Session Clerk of the Church and involved himself in the Church welfare and affairs. He was an easy and entertaining conversationalist and corresponded avidly with many people, including some famous men of his time.

It was while Robert Jamieson was at Whiteness that his talent for writing became apparent. He wrote for journals in the North of Scotland, became a contributor to the local press once it was established in Shetland and was later involved in writing for the national press. From 1869 to 1872 in the context of discussion of the Education Act, he wrote a series of papers to the London Times which were said considerably to have influenced public opinion on this issue. It has been difficult positively to identify articles as being his as many of his writing were attributed 'Anon'.

In 1858 he was appointed to his old school Cruisdale, Sandness. This was a more lucrative post and he was attracted to his birthplace, despite it being remote from the centre of education. Cruisdale was pronounced "kroosdal". The name may have originated from "kro" a knee or knob as the house stood on a stoney outcrop. There was a shallow valley below which might account for the "dal".

In the 19th century the appeals for parochial (legal) schools were put to and passed by the Church of Scotland General Assembly and the "General Assembly schools" were founded. One such school was in Tingwall at which, in 1849, Robert Jamieson attended a meeting of the Shetland teachers to discuss the formation of a local branch of the Educational Institute of Scotland. There he met Barbara Laing whom he married in 1861. She was the eldest daughter of Robert Laing, the schoolmaster of Gulberwick and his wife Christina Laurenson. The Laing family were related to an Orcadian family, the Laings, one of whom, Samuel, was the earliest translator into English of Snorre Sturlason Heimskringla or King's of Norway.

The marriage between Barbara Laing and Robert Jamieson produced eight children, six boys and two girls. Three of the boys became medically qualified. E. B. Jamieson was the seventh child.

Barbara, Mrs Robert Jamieson, inherited her father's intellect and was as well read in general literature as her husband. By her kind understanding she had great influence over the people of Sandness, being of them and therefore much more to them than the Laird's lady or the Minister's wife.

Robert's house and the schoolroom at Cruisdale, Sandness was an old thatched building little bigger than a barn, dilapidated, with a leaking roof and an earth floor. Having been built as a croft house, it was quite inadequate for a family and over 60 pupils. The Society for Promoting Christian Knowledge paid the salaries of its teachers and for the provision of school text books, but had not power to fund the erection of school buildings. These had to be provided by the community as Cruisdale was not a parochial school where the heritors would have been obliged to contribute.

Robert Jamieson was granted an acre of land at Cruisdale on which to build his schoolhouse by the Laird of the Melbie Estate, a Dr R. T. C. Scott who had previously been a naval surgeon, retired with the rank of "deputy director of hospitals and fleets". Dr Scott was a very genial, cultured man of his time and he had the vision of a prosperous and contented tenantry. His granting of the acre of land to Robert Jamieson may, in fact have been an illegal transaction, as Dr Scott was not a hereditary Laird.

Through the editors of the papers for which he wrote Robert Jamieson had come in touch with affluent, philanthropic people in the South. From 1869 he wrote many "begging" letters both to people in Shetland, Scotland and England and obtained a favourable response. In a few years, by the generosity of those people, from Baroness Burdett-Coutts downwards, he collected the sum of £500. For this sum the school and schoolhouse at Cruisdale were built. Some of the donors remained corresponding friends for the rest of Robert Jamieson's life. His appeal for the school at Cruisdale was supported by his friend and associate of many years, Archibald Nichol, the minister of the parish of Walls and Sandness.

In February 1869 his letter in the *Glasgow Herald* sought one shilling (5p) from each of the parochial schoolmasters in Scotland. His letter of appeal, for funds to complete the project was sent outwith Shetland with his Ministers's supporting letter.

Whilst the old school was being pulled down and the new one built, Mr Jamieson transferred his pupils to the United Free Church. In 1870 the new school and schoolhouse at Cruisdale was built to standards which anticipated those demanded in the Education Act of 1872. Amongst the contributors to the school was a retired merchant who had made his fortune in Madras. This man whose name was believed to be John Kay stipulated that the school was to be named "Madras School". When completed Robert Jamieson's school was officially named "Sandness Madras School" which it remained from 1870 to 1899. Another suggestion about the origin of the name of the school is that contributions were also obtained from the Trustees of Dr Andrew Bell, which trust also assisted in the foundation of Madras College at St Andrews. The Madras system utilised in the Madras schools originated in India and employed the senior pupils to help teach the youngsters.

The project was successful despite local opposition stated, in his obituary in *The Shetland Times*, to have arisen from "ignorance, indolence, jealousy, misapprehension, stupidity and wrong-headedness". However, once the school was completed and functioning successfully Robert Jamieson and his educational achievement were greatly appreciated. Robert's academic potential may have been limited by his complete loyalty and determination to continue working at the Sandness School. His abilities could have led him much further afield, though his health had been permanently taxed by the fight to establish the new school. He did however, from the time the school came under state supervision in 1874, achieve annually favourable reports from the school inspectors.

The Sandness School provided infant, primary and effectively senior secondary education for 100 children. The school educated a large number of future captains in the British Merchant Navy and Robert Jamieson's own sons went directly from Sandness School to University. Robert Jamieson was remembered by former pupils as a dignified man who was physically and intellectually massive. He was actually only 5'6" in height but his chest measurement was 46". He was widely read and brought a clear philosophical mind to bear on most subjects. He was a kind and generous host and despite his usually serious disposition could on occasions exhibit a bright and infectious sense of humour.

The first half an hour of the Sandness school day was devoted to scripture, when selected portions of the Bible were read. All pupils memorised the Ten Commandments. Memory training was emphasised in the rest of the curriculum by the memorising of tables, spellings, pieces of poetry and chosen passages from English literature. The pupils were also asked to repeat pieces of verbal instructions that they had been given. After scripture came the "three R's", english composition, history and geography, each in short periods. There was a belief that there was a short receptive period in a child's mind for any one thing and that children therefore became more obtuse after lengthy periods of exposure to a subject. Book-keeping was offered to pupils who desired it and to potential young seamen, Robert also taught the elements of navigation. A letter from J. P. S. Jamieson, Robert and Barbara's youngest child, recalls such potential seamen learning to use a quadrant and poring over "Norie's Tables".

Jamieson used local topography to illustrate geographical terms but he was recalled to be totally ignorant of Botany and utterly to discount Darwinian evolution. Discipline was maintained largely by verbal reproof. The tawse were kept in evidence, hanging up in full view, but were very rarely used. Boys who had been insubordinate or dishonest were chastised on the palm of the outstretched hand. Quite often a rebuke was conveyed by a half humorous remark which turned the laughter of the other pupils on the delinquent. Discipline was easy because misbehaviour was just not popular. It was also discipline by public opinion of the pupils.

Robert Jamieson had his school built before the 1872 Education Act. There was provision in the Act for "voluntary" schools to be carried on under departmental annual inspection and these received grants based on average daily attendance and on the merit of work done as assessed by the inspector. Robert Jamieson chose to be in this class of school rather than to come under a local school board. Everyone was satisfied for it avoided both the expense of building a further school and the attendant expenditure from the rates.

The Sandness Madras School was run by the Jamieson family. This ensured that whatever grants were made to the school establishment, by the education department, remained within the family. With a pupil role of 64 the income was £158. Each of the Jamiesons and other bright students on reaching the age of 14 became a pupil teacher. This may explain why the Jamieson children did not, as would have been expected, go to the Anderson Educational Institute. Mrs Jamieson taught the girls sewing and singing. Christina taught for part of the day and each of the six sons served his four years as pupil teacher. Robert Jamieson was known locally as "da master", and Barbara Jamieson as "da mistress".

Parish schoolmasters of that time maintained their families by crofting. The school hours were short, ten till half past two in winter, leaving time for the croft work. They had their own cows, hence butter and milk, hens providing eggs, sheep yielding mutton and were able to supplement their diet by the fish they caught. Though the Sandness schoolhouse was like a barracks the family were well nourished in this way. Snarraness and Sandness were both well cultivated and self-supporting having a few lambs and a pig.

As youngsters the Jamieson children would walk long distances. They were all fond of Shetland folklore and they would recite the familiar stories as they walked as well as arguing and discussing. In the evenings the family would complete the *Observer* crossword or pull chairs in front of the fire and tell stories. The tradition of story telling was largely of the Norse legends.

In addition to his teaching, reading and writing, Robert Jamieson had other duties. He was local postmaster, registrar of births, marriages and deaths, session clerk and for years an emigration agent. In those days he sent many scores of colonists to New Zealand. These activities brought him in close contact with the community as well as his pupils. The people came to rely on him for guidance on all manner of difficulties which they presented to him almost daily.

Mr Cooper, the editor of the *Scotsman*, received many books for review. At intervals he made a clearance and had cases of modern literature sent to Robert Jamieson. Friends in the south sent their copies of *Illustrated London News*, *The Graphic*, *Punch*, and other periodicals so there was an excellent selection which always included the *Times* and the *Scotsman*. All of these were freely available to the Jamieson family , the pupils and the local community. There were thus some of the elements of a free lending library.

Robert Jamieson's sudden death from asthma on the 19th December, 1899, was a loss which led to many other adverse changes for his family. There was no pension and the family were left impoverished. It was also the end of Sandness as a voluntary school.

The Parish School Board became the responsibility of the local authority. On Robert Jamieson's death six months of the school year remained. The school inspector's visit was due and there was no certificated teacher in charge as neither Christina nor any of her brothers were certificated. The school board solved the problem by appointing an aged, retired certificated teacher as a nominal "master". He was employed at 30 shillings (£1.50p) a week to teach, sign the rolls and keep a daily record of work. At the next school inspection the report was extremely glowing.

From the time that their father died John and Edward manned the longboats, cut the corn, brought in the harvest and undertook a great deal of the outside work whilst supporting the family. The family later moved to a larger house called Twageos in Lerwick which became their tribal gathering place.

The original schoolhouse at Sandness is now a heap of rubble. Across the road is a more solid building, the present well equipped schoolhouse where in 1947, 21 children were taught by two teachers, and today 12 children are taught by one teacher. This indicates the considerable reduction in population in Shetland since Robert Jamieson's time.

Robert Jamieson had educated himself and ensured education for his family and the people of Sandness. This was a great achievement in an era when education was regarded as a privilege, rarely available to the poor. The lives of many of Robert and Barbara Jamieson's children were substantially determined by the early education they had received at their father's school at Cruisdale, Sandness.

FRANCIS ROBERT JAMIESON, (1862–1927)

FRANCIS, the eldest son of Robert and Barbara, was E. B. Jamieson's oldest sibling. He was a kind and gentle man, loved by his family and he succeeded his father as the guiding spirit in the family.

When he first went to university in Edinburgh there were no roads from his home and Francis, as other Shetland students, walked to the ferry carrying his goods on his back. These included a barrel of meal to ensure his sustenance during term time.

The needs of many such students were recognised and provided for by the University of Edinburgh in the "Meal Monday" mid-term holiday. Students used this holiday weekend to return home for further supplies of meal which ensured their nutrition for the remainder of the term. This holiday was only abolished by the university court in the academic year 1967/68.

As a student Francis was a prominent and active member of the Student Representative Council. He was very involved in the tricentenary celebrations of Edinburgh University in 1883. He was also prominent in the election campaigns for the post of rector. The rector, a special officer of Scottish universities, is elected by the student body and thereby becomes chairman of the university court. Francis Jamieson's contribution was to write election literature, with the writing of campaign verse being his particular skill.

He achieved a first class honours in classics and mental philosophy and after graduation gained the Baxter Classical Scholarship for £300. This was an extraordinary achievement for a boy who came to Edinburgh with a vast background in British literature but no knowledge of Greek. After graduation, aged 21 years, he was invited to teach in the University College at Dundee. Having worked there for only one summer, he returned to Edinburgh University, initially as an assistant lecturer in the department of humanity and later lecturer in Latin literature to the Edinburgh Association for the University Education of Women. In those days, in the ancient Scottish universities, the department of humanity was the equivalent of the department of Latin in other universities. Latin literature was the responsibility of a lecturer within that department. Professor William Sellar held the chair from 1863 to 1890 and regarded Francis as a son. Following Professor Sellar's death many wanted Francis to apply for the chair but he felt he was too young. When Harry Chester Goodhart was elected to the chair of humanity (1891–95), Francis was assistant and later lecturer in Latin literature. He also taught junior humanity.

As a lecturer he was a favourite with students as a source of good advice and also through his interest in the social life of the university. There was great regard for his scholarship, tact and care with students as individuals. In spite of student support Francis did not get the chair following Professor Goodhart's death. The reason was said to be that he did not have an Oxford or Cambridge degree. It must have been particularly galling to Francis, considering the huge workload that he had endured, particularly when, being too old to serve in the 1914–18 war, he took on the running of the department. During Professor Goodhart's fatal illness and for a while thereafter he was substitute professor, taught and lectured three hours a day and also looked after three classes. He was by nature a workaholic.

Goodhart's successor was William Ross Hardie (MA Edinburgh 1880, Balliol College, Oxford : BA 1884, MA 1887). Professor Hardie was a strong advocate of the Scottish tradition, spoke vernacular Scots and was active in promoting the chair of Celtic in the university. Professor Hardie and Francis were good friends.

Francis' character may be demonstrated by his role in an investigation into the behaviour and habits of a professor. Francis was asked to give evidence to the university court. His kindliness must have prevailed as the professor was not censured but merely adjudged to be eccentric.

Towards the end of this period Francis Jamieson began, though never completed, studies for the Scottish Bar. The legal studies were, however, of value in the next phase of his career. In 1896 he was appointed to be one of Her Majesty's Inspectors of Schools. When he left the university, the students' council arranged on the 18th February, 1897, their presentation to him of a massive silver jardiniere. It was a great occasion, with Professor Hardie presiding, the printed programme contained a photograph of Mr Francis Jamieson and there was singing by two students accompanied on the piano.

In this new post he worked first in Glasgow, then Dumfries and Galloway, Argyle and later Lanarkshire. In October 1903 he came to Edinburgh where he stayed for the remainder of his working life. In 1910 he became chief inspector for the Southern Division of Scotland. He was awarded an LL.D from Edinburgh University in 1924.

He was married twice, first to Grace Haswell, who died of tuberculosis. Francis and his second wife, Lucy Stowell, were married for 18 years. They had a son Francis Stowell and a daughter Norna. Francis Stowell (1908–1981) read classics at Magdalen College Oxford, then went into Standard Life, where he became an actuary. He served with the Seaforth Highlanders as an adjutant and was taken prisoner after the battle of El Alamain. After the war he returned to Standard Life and eventually became investments manager. He was also chairman of the board of Governers for his old school Fettes College. Norna obtained an honours degree in history at Edinburgh University in the early 1930s. From 1933–37 she trained as a nurse at St Thomas's Hospital in London. After travelling widely in the RAF from 1938–48 she returned to St Thomas's Hospital as tutor until her retirement in 1974.

Francis Jamieson was a boating enthusiast who always sailed during August. He was at one time considered to be the best oarsman in the north of Scotland.

E. B. Jamieson frequently brought some of his students, many of whom were from overseas, to Francis's Murrayfield home for Sunday supper. Francis's strong sense of extended family led him to help his younger brothers financially and practically, but the whole family operated as a mutually supportive and caring group. Each year many members of the family met in Twageos for a family gathering.

Francis died of cancer in 1927, aged 64 years, working until five days before his death. After his death, his brother John Jamieson, took over Francis's supportive position in the family.

CHRISTINA JAMIESON (1864–1942)

CHRISTINA Jamieson was born in the schoolhouse of Cruisdale in Sandness, the second child and eldest daughter of Robert and Barbara Jamieson. She had no academic qualifications but was talented and became a notable Shetland woman, a well known public figure, author and a recognised authority on the history and sociology of Shetland.

As she grew up Christina, like her six brothers, assisted her father, the dominie, by teaching in his school. Following the death of her father the family left the schoolhouse, to live in accommodation which faced the Queen's Hotel on South Commercial Street, Lerwick. Later they accepted the tenancy of Twageos House, also in Lerwick.

Christina was intensely interested in the traditions of Shetland. This knowledge of the activities and way of life of the Shetlanders was recorded in her articles for *The Peoples Journal, The Scotsman* and *The Weekly Scotsman* between

1899 and 1904. She regretted the rapid disappearance of Shetland's rich social tradition and was very active in efforts to preserve the individual customs and practices of its various communities.

She wrote articles about diverse aspects of Shetland social and working life and the islands art and craft, indicating the differences in life for men, women and children. She also wrote short stories both under her own name and under the pen name of John Cranston. A John Cranston story in *The Weekly Scotsman* of 18th August, 1894, was "Maichie's Ride", a Shetland smuggling story.*

Christina was the first woman to hold office on public boards in Shetland. Her first appointment was to Lerwick's School Board in 1916 of which she became chairwoman in 1918 while the chairman was serving in the war. He resumed the chair when he returned to civilian life though she continued to serve on the board in its various forms until 1922. She also was on the County of Zetland Insurance Committee. She was a Scottish Women's Rural Institute (SWRI) lecturer.

She, like her father, was troubled all her life by a chronic chest problem, probably asthma, though this did not reduce her effectiveness as a housekeeper. Her hospitality was generous, especially to the students whom E. B. Jamieson brought to Shetland from Edinburgh.

She took a homely, kind interest in many projects. Her keen intellect and precision were impressive, which, coupled with good conversational powers, serenity, common sense and humour, made her a woman of rare charm and distinction.

During the 1920s a group of young people led by Alex Johnston, who came from the island of Papa Stour formed a concert party. This was in part to preserve old tunes, songs and dances in addition to well authenticated plays describing historical events in Shetland. They required quite spacious accommodation and these needs, for rehearsals and writings, were amply provided, on three or four evenings a week, by Christina Jamieson's big kitchen at Twageos.

Christina, her nephew Robert who lived with her, and other members of the Jamieson family were a fund of knowledge for the concert party. Some of Christina's stories were rewritten as plays by members of the group, and played at Shetland evenings, in the typical dress of each parish, in village halls throughout the country districts. Christina would also act in these performances.

This group was the origin of the Shetland Folklore Society, which involved 50 or more members. Fiddlers played old Shetland Dances including the ancient Sword Dance of Papa Stour revived by Alex Johnston. Other Shetland dances were also revived, "The Foula Reel" and the various versions of the Shetland Reel, "The Pin Reel" and "The Muckle Reel O'Finnigart". They also gave garden

* See Appendix 1

parties which proved to be very popular and included a memorable visit from the Faroes in 1930.

When the Scottish Community Drama Association sponsored a drama festival in Lerwick, Christina wrote a play *Da Dooble Sporin* for the occasion. This was acted by the Shetland Folklore Society and won first prize and special commendation. Christina was also a poet, using the Shetland dialect. A notable poem was "My Native Land". She had an ambition to write a "Shetland Book", similar to the "Orkney Book", but though such a book was published in the 1960s, Christina was not involved.

As a member of the non-militant suffragette movement, Christina campaigned and wrote on behalf of the cause and also helped establish the Shetland branch before the 1914–18 war. The design and construction of a large suffragette banner which was paraded at a mass demonstration in London was, in part, the product of her activities. She invited a suffragette speaker, Mrs Snowden, to speak in Lerwick.

There is a very touching letter written by Christina in 1906, to a Dr Washbourn which reveals may aspects of her personality. Henry Everley Arthur Washbourn first matriculated aged 24 years in the academic session 1899–1900 at Edinburgh University Medical School. He was born in Nelson, New Zealand, graduated MB. ChB with second class honours in 1905 and was awarded the MD in 1908. His thesis was entitled "Teratogenesis: a brief account of the past and present theories with special reference to Anencephal". He returned to New Zealand in 1908. He was a student friend of Jamie (J. P. S.) Jamieson who followed him to New Zealand. Henry Washbourn died on 14th June, 1947. It is not clear in what context Christina's letter came to be written, but, as it portrays something of her intellect and feelings, it is reproduced here.

I have some difficulty in adjusting myself to the altered conditions of our correspondence, and I fancy too that your metaphysical phase of mind will have altered with your environment, and you will no longer be greatly interested in abstract discussions about life and the various philosophies that help or hinder us in our struggle through it. It is curious that we all discover that we have no real free will, we all at times criticise and defend our own place in life almost as if we were responsible for the choice and structure of it. We all accept a certain amount of responsibility. And we all despise people who charge fate with their failures and misfortunes. So we do have some free will. And regarding our philosophies we are all prone to wrestle most with life's problems when we are least fit, when we are weary, depressed, disheartened. These are the times when the inexplicable presses sorest. And what is worse, most of the most abiding convictions and purposes are formed during these impropitious periods.

Besides what can one poor little ordinary human mind hope to accomplish in grappling with questions that have baffled the finest and strongest human intellects in all ages? Yet, knowing all this I too go on battering my poor muddled head against the unyielding walls of the unknowable. But I don't do it as much as I used to. And working in the gardens, playing with little children in the fields and shore and reading good novels have done more than any other agencies I know to save me from states of mind bordering on madness or at least hysteria. But I recognise that these refuges are not available to everybody.

I endorse all you say about EB's qualities, although there are some subjects on which I refuse to accept his judgment, because a man who has no appreciation of poetry has not a properly balanced brain (Not that a poetical person has one. The poetical person is usually unappreciative of other things which are essential).

But I refuse to endorse what you say about marriage. Granted that given ideal people it is an ideal state, the majority of married people are not ideal, and, that being so, there is no condition more perfectly adapted for the infliction of mutual unhappiness than marriage. Or if there is not unhappiness, what is taken for happiness is often mere comfort. And one can have comfort without marriage. Marriage is really a condition which only the very strongest love can justify, and that too when other conditions are all perfect. Many marriages are absolutely iniquitous. Besides a man's marriage is often a sign of deterioration. A man will start life with very high and pure ideals, and will make a good fight for a time. Then, finding that high standards don't pay, he will slacken down, lower his whole tone, decide that, as he is sure of no life but the present, he will take all the good out of it that he can, marry comfortably and pass on his failures and complexities to the innocent beings who love and confide in him. He says that he is doing no worse than he has been done to. But there is nothing more dastardly than to pass on a wrong, oftener by a marriage than by anything else. They may be scattered all over the world, and their sense of friendship be unimpaired, they will be in touch whenever they meet. But let their wives be uncongenial...

Moreover love, though it is most exalting and ennobling and gives one a sense of being in touch with omnipotence, is a "jealous God", and unless all its demands, which are nigh unappeasable, are fulfilled, it is a bondage, obsession, a pain. One longs for freedom, the serenity of the days when one is not in love. Friendship is far better. It is calm and reasonable and sustaining. Even the best love marriages ultimately resolve themselves into friendship.

Mind you this is not against marriage. It is against marriage on any grounds other than I have pointed out. So, we shall be delighted to see EB married, if the right wife for him can be found. But he is conceivably happy as a bachelor. Nay I can even imagine him yielding fatherly encouragement, comfort and counsel out of his large serenity of soul, to trembling mortals who start and shrink on the brink of matrimony.

I have much sympathy in what you say about the disappointing absence of good qualities in the mass of people one has to deal with. I suppose we ought to value what is potential in them. We ourselves would ask to be judged by our tendencies, rather

than our accomplishment. I think the people who should have a philosophy of life are
our mothers and they say nothing except that we are all to be kind to one another.

so the Lord be with you

Yours ever sincerely

Christina Jamieson

PS. I've reread this and I'd never have the courage to send it, if I didn't know I'll
never see you again.

Christina Jamieson's extensive fictional and philosophical writings included a pamphlet "A Sketch of Votes for Women". She later gave a lecture on this theme which was extensively quoted in *The Shetland News* of 20th March, 1909. The response was a strong letter of condemnation. The letter was headed with a note from the editor stating that "we do not hold ourselves responsible, nor associate ourselves in any way with the opinions expressed by our correspondent in this column". The correspondent begins by saying that were he to have known her, he would have committed the lecture to the fire. The lecture was adjudged to have been a failure, though he was not present. A friend who was there said the lecture lacked soul. He was said to have had to read it twice to get the drift, though he felt the text had much in common with a train timetable but lacking in accuracy. Whilst the letter was anonymous, a clue was given by the second half of the letter in which the author eulogised in relation to Christina's father whom he knew. Another clue to the identity of the anonymous writer was that he described his own life as full of sorrows and much trial. He suggested that women should cut their teeth on the drudgery of boards and other representative offices before embarking on their great loud-mouthed outcry and hysteria for the vote.

She also wrote in *The Shetland News* of 22nd and 29th January, 1910, a moving article on the plight of "The Women of Shetland". This described the history of women's rights indicating that men secure for themselves the more inspiring and productive jobs, leaving the dull, mundane jobs to women and the weaker men. When men were away at war or sea, women were allowed more freedom of activity. During the Saxon and Norman period women were allowed public and religious roles. Christina attributed the introduction of the Protestant faith as coinciding with the loss of status for women. Women were then for marriage, private life, meekness, patience and silence and to repress all personal ambition for knowledge. During the Civil War and the restoration of the monarchy, women continued their subservient role, despite women and some men writing of the need for universal education. Other men grouped women, infants, idiots and lunatics as persons unable to exercise a sound discretion in political affairs. Polite men of that time did not speak of politics in front of women.

The Reform Act of 1832 extended the franchise to all male persons, the first time such a distinction was made in British history. Such a distinction was previously unnecessary as the right to the vote was not made by gender but income. In 1847 Anne Knight, a Quaker, first voiced in print disquietude over the ineligibility of women to vote. Other educated and socially advantaged women followed and the result was the foundation of colleges and journals for women. An amendment to a Representation of the Peoples Bill, allowing women the vote was lost in Parliament in 1866. The women's suffragette movement gained momentum during the Victorian era but without immediate success.

Christina's article was written in clear and effective language, concluding with "Men are not fit, and have no right, to assume wholly to themselves the control of the destinies of women". In the copy of the tract referred to here, is a hand written addition dated 1928, "Since this was written, women have won their rights by their great services to their country and to humanity during the war".

In her old age, at about the same time as the tenancy of Twageos lapsed, Christina emigrated to New Zealand in the hope that a less rigorous climate would help her asthma. Another factor in her decision to leave was the slow decline in the numbers of the Shetland Folklore Society, leading eventually to the closure of this group's activity. In New Zealand she was active in various Shetland associations. Following her death, most of her belongings were destroyed. She was a tall striking handsome woman who may, perhaps, have felt great frustrations at the limits placed on the use of her fine intellect.

WILLIAM JAMES (1866–1920)

WILLIAM James, the second son and third Jamieson child became a large, strong, witty and kindly man, who though able, lacked ambition and application. He had no time for the academic life, but was involved in "social and not infrequently alcoholic activities". He was briefly apprenticed to legal firms, first in Edinburgh and later in Hawick but failed to sustain either. He then worked preserving meat using antiseptics. In this trade he moved to London to be able to work in the Smithfield Market. From London he went first to South Africa and then to Wellington, New Zealand.

He married twice, first to Margaret Menzies who divorced him and then to Anne Young. The child of his first marriage was a son, Bertie, who was brought up in Shetland and who came to live in Twageos House with Christina and Barbara Jamieson, his grandmother.

Bertie, like his father was not an achiever, and worked as a taxi driver in Lerwick. He died in the early 1930s, dour, withdrawn, and somewhat resentful about life. Bertie was a committed communist.

William's second family in New Zealand by Anne Young consisted of a daughter Vaila May and three sons, Douglas, Ian Francis and James Peter. This second family of William's was fostered. James Peter spent some time gold digging and then became a successful customs officer with four able children. He did a great deal of work on the Jamieson genealogy.

ROBERT, (1868–1894)

ROBERT was the third son and fourth child of the Jamiesons, about whom little is recorded. He is said to have wanted to go to sea, but for unexplained reasons did not achieve that ambition. Instead he became a commercial traveller and died, aged 26, of pneumonia.

ANNE, (1871–1921)

ANNE was the fifth child and second Jamieson daughter. She was said to be very much less intellectually endowed than her brothers and sister, though it is uncertain whether or not she suffered from a learning disability. She never achieved independence but lived with her parents and then with Christina at Twageos.

JOHN K. JAMIESON, (1873–1948)

JOHN K. Jamieson, the sixth child and fourth son of Robert and Barbara Jamieson, graduated MB ChB in Edinburgh in 1894. He was known to his friends, acquaintances and students as "Jimmy", "Jamie" or "JK".

His first post was in Surgeons Hall, Edinburgh as demonstrator in anatomy to Macdonald Brown, lecturer in the Extra-mural School of Medicine. A year later he went to work in the anatomy department at the Yorkshire College which later became Leeds University. John was first appointed assistant to the professor of anatomy, Professor Wardrop Griffiths at a nominal salary but the post did however include the office of warden of Lyddon Hall a student residency, where he had free board and lodgings.

In 1910, on Griffith's appointment to the Chair of Medicine, Jamieson was appointed the first full-time professor of anatomy. This gave him both the time and opportunity for teaching and lecturing particularly on anatomical dissection. In tune with the times, he believed that a sound training in human anatomy was the only true basis for clinical work. His blackboard drawings were superb. He could draw a symmetrical thorax using both hands at the same time and it was said that he could draw a perfect circle whilst standing sideways to the blackboard, swinging his arms round. This always raised a cheer and, with a graceful lifting of his hand he would indicate that the cheering should stop. He taught anatomy as form in relation to function, but when asked by Lord

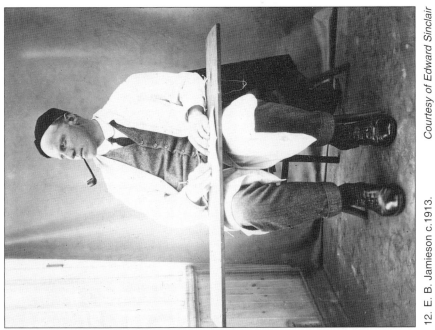

12. E. B. Jamieson c.1913.

11. E. B. Jamieson in skull cap.

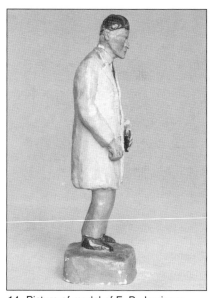

13. John K. Jamieson, reprinted from "The Daily Chronicle", 28.01.1926.

14. Picture of model of E. B. Jamieson.

15. Bill Dawson, Wilfie Jackson and E. B. Jamieson in Shetland. *Courtesy of Edward Sinclair*

16. E. B. Jamieson with three students at East Beach, Snarraness.

Courtesy of Edward Sinclair

17. E. B. Jamieson carrying a lamb, Papa Stour. *Courtesy of Edward Sinclair*

18. E. B. Jamieson with (l-r) Jimmy and Johnie Sinclair.

Courtesy of Edward Sinclair

20. E. B. Jamieson, c.1943. This photograph, taken by one of his students so pleased E. B. J. that he used reproductions on which he conveyed his Christmas greetings.

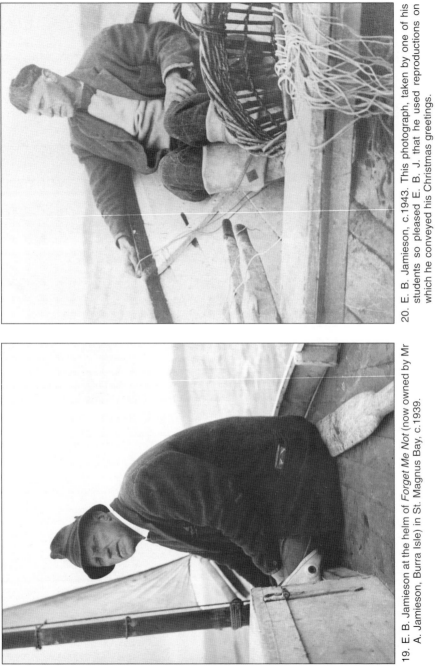

19. E. B. Jamieson at the helm of *Forget Me Not* (now owned by Mr A. Jamieson, Burra Isle) in St. Magnus Bay, c.1939.

21. Snarraness in 1998.

Gluteus med m
(cut near orig)

Gluteus minim m

Tensor fasciae latae m

Gluteus med m
(cut near ins)

Inf glut a and
n (L5 S1 2)

Obtur ext m

Post fem cut
n (S1 2 3)

Quadratus fem m

Sciatic n on
add mag m

Gluteus maxim m
ins iliotib tract

Long head
biceps fem m

Tend erector
spinae m

Post sup iliac spine

Sup glut a and
n (L4 5 S1)

Piriformis m

Int pudend a and
pudend n (S2 3 4)

Perf cut n (S2 3)
and sacrotub lig

Tend obtur int
m, gemelli and
n to obtur int m
(L5 S1 2)

Orig
semimembranosus m

Transv br med
circumflex a and
n to hamstrings

Semitendinosus m

Add mag m

Gracilis m

Gluteal Region I

22. Anatomical drawing from E. B. Jamieson's *Illustrations of Regional Anatomy*, E. & S. Livingstone, Edinburgh, 1934. (Refer to text on facing page).

Gluteal Region

Landmarks to be Identified. - Greater trochanter. Iliac crest; posterior superior iliac spine. Sacrum and coccyx; sacro-tuberous lig.; ischial tuberosity. Fold of the buttock. Borrders of gluteus maximus; gluteal tuberosity.

    Superficial Fascia of Gluteal Region. 1. Loaded with *fat*. Tough and stringy over ischial tuberosity.

    Contains also : 2. Small *unnamed arteries* that come through the deep fascia from the deep arteries.

3. Corresponding *veins*.

4. *Lymph-vessels.*

5. Numerous cutaneous nerves.

    Lymph-vessels end in the glands of the groin - superficial inguinal lymph-glands.

    Posterior branch of lateral cutaneous nerve of thigh turns downwards and backwards into the lower lateral part of the re-gion.

    Lateral cutaneous branch of subcostal nerve (12th thoracic) appears through the deep fascia at the iliac crest immediately in front of the tubercle of the crest and descends in the anterior or lateral part of the region as far as the greater trochanter.

    Lateral cutaneous branch of ileo-hypogastric appears just behind the tubercle and descends for a like distance.

    Cutaneous branches of *posterior primary rami* of the **upper three lumbar nerves** appear a little above the highest point of the iliac crest and descend almost to the fold of the buttock.

    Cutaneous branches of posterior primary rami of the upper three sacral nerves, having pierced gluteus maximus, appear through the deep fascia between the posterior superior iliac spine and the coccyx (about an inch apart) and ramify in the medial part of the region.

    Perforating cutaneous nerve arises in pelvis from anterior primary rami of S.2 and 3, perforates sacro-tuberous lig., gluteus maximus and deep fascia about midway between coccyx and ischial tuberosity, and ramifies in the lower medial part of the region.

    Two or three *gluteal branches* of **posterior cutaneous nerve of thigh** curve round the middle third of lower border of gluteus maximus, pierce the deep fascia and supply the lower part of the region.

    Deep Fascia. - Extends up from the back of the thigh; splits to enclose gluteus maximus; gives partial origin to it, and sends septa into it to divide it into coarse bundles. Above and in front of the gluteus maximus, where the fasciae covers the antero-superior part of gluteus medius, it is greatly thickened and is continuous with the ileo-tibial tract.

    Muscles and Ligaments. - Gluteus maximus, medius and minimus; piriformis; obturator internus and two gemilli; quadratus femoris; obturator externus. Sacro-spinous and sacro-tuberous ligs.

    Sacro-Tuberous Lig. - A long, strong band, wider at its ends than in the middle. Hidden by the lower medial part of gluteus maximus, part of which arises from it. *Upper end* attached to the posterior iliac spines and to sacrum and coccyx. *Lower end* attached to the lower medial impression on ischial tuberosity.

Moynihan, the great Leeds surgeon if a certain operation would be possible, John replied that the limitations of surgery were physiological not anatomical.

As with his brother E. B. Jamieson, he taught in the great Edinburgh anatomy tradition, the lectures were carefully prepared and delivered, always accompanied by simple diagrams. Again like E. B. Jamieson, John's lectures were virtually the same every year, including the jokes. He was also a conscientious attender in the dissecting room sitting with students, teasing out the various anatomical features.

His great kindliness was a feature of his student contact and he was a great success as a teacher and examiner. He wanted to know whether the student understood the make up of the body rather than requiring a precise knowledge of the name of the structure. He asked the anxious student up for his oral and practical examination in anatomy to locate particular structures rather than to name an indicated structure. He was known as the students' friend. In later life students still kept in touch with him. He usually responded to their letters by return.

John Jamieson was an authority on the lymphatic system. In his classical work he was closely involved with J. F. Dobson and Moynihan, his friendship with both dated from when he was a demonstrator in anatomy. They described the surgical anatomy of the lymphatic system draining the testicle, tongue, stomach and large intestine. The thin walled lymphatics are difficult to identify at dissection. Their surgical interest lies in their importance in the spread of disease, in particular cancer.

When John Jamieson was appointed to the chair of anatomy, there was little or no administrative responsibility outside the department. However in 1914, the then dean, De Burgh Birch, the professor of physiology was mobilised with his territorial regiment. John Jamieson was appointed acting dean for the next three years.

In March 1915 he was commissioned as major and appointed registrar at the East Leeds Hospital in Beckett Street. In 1917 he was promoted to lieutenant colonel and became the very able administrator of his hospital. He particularly relished his contact and involvement in the well-being of the non-commissioned officers and men. After the war he regularly attended the reunions of the men in his unit.

The remainder of his life was devoted to academic administration, of which he was a master. He had the ability to make a number of individuals of diverse character and interest work as an effective team. He was seen as a rock of reliability in an ever changing world. He was elected Dean of the faculty of medicine and chairman of its board in 1918, and held this post for a record 18 years. Within the university during his period as dean, he was on the University Council and the finance, salaries and estates committee. He was pro-vice-chancellor from 1923 to 1925 and acting vice-chancellor during 1923–24. He was involved also as an external examiner throughout the land and was a member of the General Medical Council. He did much to promote further education for nurses. Leeds was the first university to give a diploma of nursing.

He was an important member of the academic group who worked to promote the Yorkshire College into the fully constituted University of Leeds. There were developments in the School of Medicine in the period between the wars, including important building programmes. The department of pathology building owed much to the generosity of Sir Algernon Firth, a gift in which John Jamieson played some part.

In 1936, as he approached retirement age, he was offered and accepted the chair of anatomy in Trinity College Dublin. His mother having heard that he was moving from Leeds to Trinity was quoted as saying, "I don't know when that boy will settle down". The course at Trinity College was a replica of the great Edinburgh anatomy course and had been developed by his predecessors. John Jamieson was successful in the difficult task of reducing the course from eight to five terms. Anatomy had for generations been the basis of medical knowledge. Every anatomy department in the world had to undergo this reduction in time and perhaps in significance to allow for the expansion of the developing disciplines of physiology and biochemistry.

Dublin was a success academically and socially for John. He was elected a Fellow of the Royal Irish Academy. He was known as a loyal friend, a wise counsellor and a genial and most hospitable host. He was an ardent golfer and freemason. He died some eight months after retirement in Black Rock, Co Dublin at the age of 75 years.

John had married Elizabeth Goodworth of Winterton in Lincolnshire in 1906, their marriage ending with Elizabeth's death in 1936. They had two children, John and Barbara. John junior was a doctor who had periods of great hardship as a prisoner-of-war both in Greece and Germany. He subsequently became Senior School Medical Officer in Leeds.

Barbara, who had a BSc from Kings College London became dietitian to the Royal Masonic Hospital, London and secretary to the British Dietetic Association. After her mother's death, Barbara gave up the post to keep house for her father, which she did for the remainder of his life. Subsequently she lived in Buckinghamshire. She was awarded an MBE for her contribution to dietetics.

J. P. S. JAMIESON, (1885–1963)

JAMES Peter Speid Jamieson was the eighth and youngest child of Robert and Barbara Jamieson. He attended and then taught in his father's school and, in the fullness of time, travelled to Edinburgh to study for an MA.

In an autobiographical note he describes his depression following the changes and the enormous work entailed in moving the family home from Cruisdale to Lerwick. He stated that he become "overdone and flat". He lived through the winter of 1899 in a blank despair. The one point of encouragement was a generous compliment from Alexander William Mair the professor of Greek in relation to James' efforts in that subject. The grim winter passed and encouraged by the family support he returned to Edinburgh. He was met by E. B. Jamieson, who greeted him with the words, "I think you would do better in medicine". His elder brother then financed James through medicine.

The change in subject was a success. Though the medical course was hard work James found it enjoyable. He worked for distinction but never attained that honour. The only distinction he achieved was to answer every one of Sir William Turner's questions in his famous senior examinations. This had only been done once before. Sir William remarked at the end, "I thought that I had him, but I didn't". In 1904 he won the Pattison prize for surgery, £24. This paid for a visit to study maternity at Coombe Hospital, Dublin. The area, a terrible slum, was close to the Guinness brewery where the men received six pints of Guinness a day in addition to their wages.

In August 1906 he had his last month's holiday at Twageos. James had considered a university appointment perhaps in physiology when his mother made one of her deeply simple remarks. She said she had three doctor sons of who two had accepted university appointments. She thought it was time that one son turned to the care of sick people.

After graduation he became class assistant to F. M. Caird, the professor of clinical surgery, who developed major abdominal surgery in Edinburgh. James duties were to prepare the lecture theatre for the day's lectures, set out specimens on the rostrum, clean the board of chalk after lectures and similar menial tasks.

For a year he was a resident surgeon at £100 per annum in the Seaman's Hospital and Dispensary in Ramsgate. There he made friends with J. B. Johnston who later became a significant figure at Guy's Hospital, London.

In 1906–1907 he became Caird's resident surgeon at the Royal Infirmary. In those days the residency in the Royal Infirmary was an expensive experience, for the resident doctors were not only unpaid but had to pay their own mess expenses. There were 20 doctors in the residency, a series of rotating officers ranging from mess president downwards. By the end of the winter of 1906 James Jamieson had exhausted his finances.

Professor Caird facilitated his appointment as medical officer to a South African gold complex. He was to earn £30 a month, have a house and a free return fare by boat. The appointment was to care for 8,000 Japanese, 1,000 Chinese and 1,000 Africans who lived in square enclosures, called compounds. There were six doctors working there, each with a ward, the hospital being managed by an ex-army sergeant. He had an older qualified assistant with a whisky cough, a qualified dispenser, a good Scots housekeeper and African servants. James Jamieson lived in Germiston. All day and night could be heard the rumblings and explosions of the mining works beneath. A large searchlight swept the area of the hospital and staff quarters. It was a dangerous place, every man carried a pistol which he kept under his pillow at night. There was a co-ordinated attack by a gang of Chinese workmen whose intention was to liberate the Chinese labourers. When the mutiny was overcome, it became apparent that the Chinese authorities were displeased. The ringleaders were executed in China.

On one occasion he was, for a while, mistaken for Dr Jameson of the famous Jameson raid and given suitable, if temporary, honours. The Jameson raid was one of the contributory events which led to the Boer War in South Africa. The raid was in 1895 - a march by 800 British soldiers lead by Dr Leander Starr Jameson into the Boer held Transvaal. It was unauthorised and unsuccesful.

James's plan was to return to Britain with his savings and become a surgeon. Instead he met Sister Janet Milligan Boddon, and the plan was abandoned. Much of South Africa was Boer, and James decided that it was better to move to New Zealand where the inhabitants were more familiar. Janet followed and arrived on 8th November to be married three days later. Dr Henry Washbourn (of Christine Jamieson's letter) gave the bride away. The wedding breakfast was at 6p.m. and the bridegroom sang Widdicombe Fair.

James first went, in 1915, to a practice in Collingwood in the Nelson district of New Zealand where there was an opening in what was called "a horse and buggy" practice. This was followed by a term of seven years in Eketahuna. He then moved to Nelson to be the resident surgeon to the Nelson Public Hospital. He held this post for five years, when he took up private practice in the city. It was rumoured that his nickname was "Guinea a grunt".

He was, however, a meticulous doctor, always striving to learn. He audited therapy and care with careful attention to diagnosis in life and post mortems after death. He proceeded to MD in 1930 and in the same year was elected a Fellow of the Royal Australasian College of Surgeons. In 1917–26 and 1932–38 he was an examiner at the Otago University Medical School. During the Second World War he was regional medical officer for the military forces for the Nelson district. James Jamieson had wide interests in the affairs of Nelson. He was a director of the Cook Strait Airways Corporation and president of the Nelson Aero Club.

He was very involved in the British Medical Association, was chairman of the Nelson division for a long period and became Dominion president in 1938. He had the great distinction of receiving a gold medal from the British Medical Association in 1949. He was also awarded Commander of the Order of the British Empire in 1956.

He was involved in medical politics and the inception of changes in the New Zealand Health service following the election of a Labour government in 1935. The stated intent was to eliminate private practice and the suggestion was that their intention was to nationalise medicine. James had the difficult task of keeping a united front with the profession and dealing with politicians and managers with a constraining schedule. He was the leader of the profession and gave up practice during this period to travel the country. Frustrations included meeting with the minister to discuss a document submitted seven months earlier to find that it had not been read. The BMA were called for consultation two evenings before the Parliamentary Bill was discussed with no previous knowledge of its content. It was said that many of the good features of the NHS in New Zealand owed much to the endeavours of James and his BMA colleagues.

James Jamieson was a meticulous and organised collector of the papers which related to his life's work. In 1992 when J. B. Lovell-Smith was writing his book *The New Zealand Doctor and the Welfare State* the author stayed with James Jamieson for a week reading through the carefully kept papers. Each evening, at precisely 5p.m., the old man would come with a bottle of whisky, a different brand each day, two glasses and a small jug of water. After clearing his throat in a characteristic manner, he admitted that his invariable custom at this hour was to have two glasses of whisky and would Lovell-Smith join him. James Jamieson's conversation was deliberate, ordered, concise and enlightened by mordant wit and a keen sense of irony. The conversation could drift from Norse legends to astronauts, from sylviculture (his hobby) to Thomas Paine. For many years he had an interest in forestry with a modest experiment with a pine plantation in the Moutere Hills inland from Nelson.

James was seen as a man with many interests, wide knowledge and the possessor of an acute intelligence in dealing with any problem. He and his wife Janet had five children, each of whom married and had children.

His eldest son, Edward became an orthopaedic surgeon at Addenbrookes Hospital Cambridge, New Zealand. He was a very good doctor as well as being an able surgeon. Former patients have visited him in New Zealand. Roger, James' second son became an aeronautical engineer and pilot in the RAF during the 1939–45 war, through which he came unscathed.

PART III
E. B. JAMIESON

THE ANATOMIST

EDWARD Bald Jamieson (1876-1956) — the fifth son and seventh child of Robert and Barbara Jamieson — announced at the age of 14 that he was not interested in an academic life. He said that he wanted an office job which would finish at 5p.m. and give him free evenings. Despite this in 1894 he was sent, against his will, to Edinburgh University where his imagination was immediately and permanently engaged. As a student he showed no special talent but graduated MB ChB Edinburgh University in 1900, his only distinction being one class medal.

Following graduation he became a demonstrator in anatomy under Professor Sir William Turner, who had a most stimulating influence on all his staff. After holding an assistantship and a lectureship for short periods, he became a senior lecturer in anatomy in 1909, a position which he held for 36 years. He continued to teach during the war, thus he worked for nearly 45 years with a series of distinguished anatomists including Cunningham, Arthur Robinson, J. C. Brash and Auckland Geddes.

He did little or no research, being involved principally in teaching, which was by accurate and succinct description. E. B. Jamieson's main interest was in topographic anatomy. He had an unusual ability in dissection of the human body and had an impressive memory for detail.

He was a member of the small subcommittee of the Anatomical Society which, in 1917, compiled the *Birmingham Revision of the Basle Nomina Anatomica*. Subsequently in 1928 he was appointed by the Anatomical Society along with A. F. Dixon and T. B. Johnston to be a member of the committee to consider a further revision.

His chief original work was the development of ordinary dissection methods for the display of the gross structure of the brain. As a young man, he performed a series of beautiful dissections of the hand and brain and annotated them with his descriptions and comments. He presented these in a MD thesis which was awarded with gold medal. At the first International Conference of Anatomy in Geneva in 1905, he gave a demonstration of various tracts of fibres and masses of grey matter of the brain displayed by ordinary dissection. In 1908 he published a description of some anomalies of nerves arising from the lumbar plexus of the foetus and of the bilaminar musculus pectineus in the same foetus.

E. B. Jamieson's main contribution to anatomical literature was in the writing of textbooks and atlases. His writings included, in 1928 a book with Professor Arthur Robinson entitled *Surface Anatomy*, in 1937 a second edition of Dixon's *Manual of Human Osteology* and a section on Osteology in the fifth to eighth editions of *Cunningham's Textbook of Anatomy*. He was also responsible with Professor J. C. Brash for the ninth and tenth Edition of Cunningham's *Manual of Practical Anatomy*.

He is perhaps best known for his *Illustrations of Regional Anatomy*. Each section of the dissection is presented in a separate volume; *Upper Limb*; *Thorax*; *Abdomen and Pelvis*; *Lower Limb* and *Head and Neck*. The volumes are known affectionately as "Jimmy's Plates". His lectures were incorporated into a compact book *Companion to Manuals of Practical Anatomy*, ("Wee Jimmy") which appeared first in 1913 and reached a seventh edition in 1950 . The dedication was to "Sir William Turner KCB, FRS whose stimulating teaching always made anatomy an interesting study." These two books were clear expositions of human anatomy. They, with the dissection of the body, were to form part of a triad to be learnt by generation of students in the anatomy room, at home or lodgings and in the medical school library. Illustrations of his writing in *A Companion to Manuals of Practical Anatomy*, Oxford University Press, ("Wee Jimmy") and the sample plates are shown in the photo section of this book.

THE TEACHER AND LEGEND

ANATOMY was, particularly until the 1960s, the principle discipline upon which clinical training and practice was based. A good grounding in anatomy was essential for a graduate in medicine.

E. B. Jamieson as a teacher of anatomy spent long periods in the dissecting room, where he was impressive. A Shetlander by birth, the Shetland of his childhood was immersed in folklore. He looked more like a Viking God who had bridged the centuries than an anatomist of the early 20th century. When he taught anatomy in Edinburgh University Medical School he used a story telling technique where, for example the course of the ulna nerve substituted for the exploits of Olaf the Nervous in Shetland historical folklore.

He alone continued the earlier practice wherein all teaching staff wore skullcaps and long white coats. He was a tall man and his second given name of Bald aptly described him. His features were impassive although capable from time to time of breaking into a warm, indeed almost mischievous, disarming smile. He had a keen sense of humour which whenever evident was universally endearing. He also had a warm personality which he did his best to hide under a gruff exterior. His voice and speech were slow and sonorous and never changed tone, pitch or volume. He moved silently around the department invariably wearing rubber soled boots and smoking a foul smelling pipe. He wore long and extremely shabby cardigans and sometimes a moleskin waistcoat. When asked why he always wore a black tie he replied that he bought one when King Edward died and he had never bothered to change it.

Recollections of him were of a genial man who had always appeared elderly. He was accepted as a great man, a man of authority and wide knowledge and yet a man who was always readily accessible and willing to be, over many years, a trusted confidant of any male student in trouble or in difficulties. E. B. Jamieson had a delight in simple things, he was remembered for his clear judgment and mode of expression which was totally free of humbug. He was outwardly austere and at times awe inspiring. To all who knew him he was, in the words of his favourite poet, Chaucer, "A varray parfait gentil knight". Perhaps he was even more akin to the Oxford cleric described in the Prologue to Chaucer's Canterbury tales.

An Oxford Cleric, still a student though,
One who had taken logic long ago,
Was there; his horse was thinner than a rake,
And he was not too fat, I undertake,
But had a hollow look, a sober stare;
The thread upon his overcoat was bare;
He had found no preferment in the church
And he was too unworldly to make search
for secular employment ...
His only care was study, and indeed
He never spoke a word more than was need,
Formal at that, respectful in the extreme,
Short, to the point, and lofty in his theme.
The thought of moral virtue filled his speech
And he would gladly learn, and gladly teach.

E. B. Jamieson's contact with the students was at a time of their greatest anxiety, the dissection of the human body. His approach was detached but caring and extremely firm. The first incision into the skin of the leathery, obviously but hardly human corpse, was one of the key moments in the transformation from lay person to doctor. The typical Scottish medical undergraduate in those days would be a young man, sometimes a callow youth aged between 16 and 17. There were older English and overseas students. All would be feeling their way in the novel experience of becoming a doctor. The period of medical education was a secluded one, with less contact with other faculties than might have been anticipated in traditional university education. Sport, raucous Saturday nights at the students union and many hours spent memorising were more typical activities for the male medical student.

The old dissecting room in Edinburgh was an imposing sight. It was a lofty room with high ceilings, three quite massive coal fires at which students warmed themselves, roof lights, a metal gallery and two lines of tables with their formalin soaked corpses for dissection. During the dissection periods the room was filled by a bustling crowd of students who sat upon stools or stood around the tables. A few sat with their books on the table or propped on 'their body'. The dissection manuals always had a characteristic oily smell of formaldehyde unlike any other smell encountered before or since. The room was also used by less diligent characters who huddled around the fire in conversation entirely unrelated to anatomy. Presiding over this rather ghoulish scene was Jimmy. Each student paid seven shillings (35p) for his part of a body to be dissected. Jimmy collected the fee and allocated a position in the dissecting room. Often such a chance allocation resulted in lifelong friendships, having shared the experience of dissecting the body and learning its anatomy under Jimmy's eagle eye.

Jimmy's room in the anatomy department was a gloomy cell immediately beneath the staircase which lead up to the dissecting room. He would appear at the entrance of the dissecting room, and make his way steadily, silently and in a stately manner to his sanctum, a glass fronted office entirely lit from the dissecting room. Though it was not possible to discern just what Jimmy did in that room, from it he presided over the dissecting room.

For a first year student to have Jimmy watching his dissection or dissecting beside him was quite an intimidating experience. He did not suffer fools gladly. He would pause briefly at one or two of the tables. From time to time he might himself take a stool. Sometimes advising and sometimes doing a little dissecting. He would teach or question a group of students and occasionally he would pick on one student to probe the extent of the studentís anatomical knowledge. It is probable that he used this method to establish the order of merit of the upper echelons of each class.

In the second year students attended Jimmy's den. In the course of two terms he covered the whole of macroscopic human anatomy. These so called demonstrations lasted for 50 minutes, five days per week. He occasionally demonstrated surface anatomy from an anatomical specimen. Jimmy's objective was to train the visual memory. He saw anatomy as little more than an exercise in memory and a handmaiden of surgery. Central to this were his blackboard diagrams in coloured chalk. Students learned their anatomy by copying the diagrams in notebooks with coloured crayons.

The moment of truth was the "spot" examinations. These were brief, related questions about a piece of dissection, a forerunner of the multiple choice examination. Knowledge or lack of it was exposed in a brief moment; hence the panic of the students.

Each student was examined four times. The examination on the first occasion was limited to fairly narrow regions. Top marks in these exams was 10. Jimmy conducted the final examination, which covered the whole section of anatomy recently dissected for which the highest possible mark was 20. In these examinations Jimmy used a long silver plated hook with which he would identify some hidden structure. The student was asked a very few questions and the exam was over in a minute. Jimmy then retired to his sanctum and recorded the mark. Meanwhile the bewildered student who had been up most of the night working for the exam consulted his colleagues as to the accuracy of his answers.

His admonition to students who had failed an examination was: "You need to do better. Go home, find a hammer and nail your scrotum to a chair".

Jimmy ran the department with almost parental care. The system was grim and austere. Jimmy was merciless in his demands for perfection. Rarely did he relax, but when he did he was funny. He quoted from the Bible once: "Three things I know not, yea four, that are too wonderful for me: the way of an eagle in the air, the way of a serpent upon a rock, the way of a ship in the midst of the sea, and the way of a man with a maid". He confessed that he would like to add a fifth, the course of the obturator nerve.

A further territory of Jimmy's influence was the magnificent anatomy department lecture theatre with its steep slope of wooden benches and metal book-rests descending to a small lecture area. Here making a grim appearance stood Jamieson in his skullcap. The first lecture started without introduction or preamble. In one of his obituaries it was recalled "Every fact, every sentence had been tested until it found its permanent place in a web of phrases resembling the structure of nerves, organs and muscles". Due to his prodigious memory the lectures, complete with all his humorous asides and mischievous errors, were virtually identical from year to year. This was verified by one student who used the notes his mother had taken from Jimmy's lectures years previously.

Jimmy came to the lecture theatre at 9a.m. sharp accompanied by a single class card which was formally placed on the lectern. On this card was the title of the anatomical subject to be covered.

A student notorious for his late arrivals at the 9a.m. anatomy lectures was met by the sergeant servitor with a note from Jimmy which read:

"Dear 'Mr MacBloggs',

Thank you for attending my lectures which you regularly interrupt at 9.15a.m. If it would suit your convenience I will start at 9.30a.m."

Another student arrived two minutes late for his part examination. Jimmy was about to move off when he arrived redfaced and breathless. "Where have you been boy?" To which the student answered, "Oh Sir the tram was late." "In that case I should complain about your exam result to the Superintendent of the Tramways Company," replied Jimmy.

At the first lecture of the New Year, he would say "Happy New Year, Head and Neck". He revelled in the annual ritual, which rolled through the seasons. Some students followed the lecture with roughly duplicated typewritten notes in loose leafed folders which were sold by Ferriers Medical Bookshop. It was these lectures which were edited and re-arranged by Jimmy to form *The Companion to Manuals of Practical Anatomy.*

Jimmy's prowess at the blackboard with coloured chalk was renowned. The blackboard illustrations were stored behind the lecture theatre. Two or three of these were brought into each lecture by a laboratory assistant in a brown coat. In these drawings the arteries were red, the veins were blue, and nerves yellow. The muscles, bones and lymphatics were all clearly identified. This contrasted with the dissected body where all tissues whatever their nature were a uniform dark brown. The drawings were published initially in a loose leaf and later in a bound form.

In private life Jimmy could be most courteous but where anatomical nomenclature was involved, he was frank and outspoken. He could be stern when the occasion demanded disapproval. Idleness was to him the cardinal sin. The offending student was treated to a, usually beneficial, disciplinary homily.

Jimmy told the story about some boy who was not getting on with his work. Jimmy met him in the street and gave him a jolly good dressing down then realised he had reprimanded the wrong boy. Next day he sent for him to come down to his office, apologised, explained the mistaken identity. "That's alright sir but I passed on the message".

One student who failed anatomy, was Irish. Jimmy asked him, "it took your father seven years to qualify. Do you intend to take as long?" The reply was "Yes, sir, I do not think it would be decent to do so in less".

Another student E. G. Lucas was told at his first meeting with Jimmy, "your father was M. G. L. Lucas, a good student; do you likewise."

An example of the frank advice which he offered to his students is when he wrote a letter to a student who was philandering. Jimmy agreed that a good looking man should get himself some good looking sons like himself but the respectable way to do it was within marriage.

His memory was legendary. Male students when they were interviewed for the first time were treated to a prolonged stare during which he memorised another new name, face and personal characteristics. He kept an eagle eye on the career of every student in his care and was aware of the capabilities and performances of each. Jimmy never gave written testimonials but he would always speak to potential employees on behalf of students. Erstwhile students would tell him that they had not met for 20 years. He would look quizzically at them for a minute as first the surname then Christian name came to his lips with a kindly smile of recognition which held a cherished memory.

A Chinese student, Ian Wang came to Edinburgh. His father and uncle had both carried out post-graduate work in Edinburgh until 1920. He timorously entered Jimmy's den to be assigned his dissection part. Jimmy kindly put Wang at his ease by asking about any medical relations. On learning that his father and uncle had been to Edinburgh many years ago he enquired about their initials and was told one was C. Y. and the other was C. C. and amazed Ian Wang by saying: "Oh yes, in those days your father preferred to be called Wong and your uncle preferred to be called Wang".

When G. H. D. McNaught came to Jimmy's small office on the ground floor of the anatomy department he was asked his name and where he came from. McNaught told him his name and that he came from Preston and mentioned the nearby doctor who was perhaps 40 years older than himself. Jimmy said, "I remember E. G. Ray. He wore the most atrocious ties".

A. S. Duncan recalled that on hearing Duncan's name Jimmy said that "at the beginning of the century there had been a Duncan who had started medicine but that his career had been not medicine but rugby football". Duncan replied, "You are referring to my uncle A. W. Duncan who left the university after a year or two and subsequently played fullback for Scotland, and captained the Grange Cricket Team, etc".

One of the class graduating in 1936 was R. Adamson. At the end of the second year, a collection was made and as the students left the dissecting room for the last time Jimmy was given a Meerschaum pipe. He was clearly moved by the gesture. Years later Adamson met Jimmy who looked over the top of his glasses and said, "Now let me see, Adamson R., 1931–33 and it was a very good pipe".

Jimmy did not generally involve himself with the female medical students. In particular he would not lecture to girls on the female reproductive organs. He was quoted as saying that women who used to be good nurses now become bad doctors.

One girl for a bet went into the men's lecture. Jimmy said, "This lecture was intended for people wearing trousers".

One of the few anecdotes about his contact with female students was when one girl failed anatomy. Jimmy wrote to the mother who had also been a medical student in Edinburgh. He stated: "Your daughter is capable in medicine and also capable of being a social success in Edinburgh. Her exam results indicated that she is not however capable of doing both. Please make sure she makes up her mind as to which she wants to do."

An anecdote offering a different view of Jimmy was when his hat had been blown over the railing round the castle. The hat sat obstinately just out of reach of his stick. As he stood gathering strength and agility to go over the railings a young soldier came swinging down and was asked to retrieve the hat. The soldier walked on without pausing but with a facial expression indicating refusal. Then three well dressed, good looking young ladies appeared from the other direction. They saw his predicament and age. One of them scrambled over, retrieved the hat with hilarious gaiety shared by the others. He said to the young lady that if he had a moustache he would have offered to kiss her. "A kiss without a moustache," he said, "is like an egg without salt." "Oh never mind that," said she, and kissed him fair and square in broad daylight in the open street to the great hilarity of the others.

Jimmy first lived in St Giles House, a former student residence owned by the Town and Gown Association. This was situated by the Old Scotsman Steps about 50 yards east of the Bank of Scotland head office. Jimmy acted as unofficial head of the house and general advisor to all student residents. He moved from there to Ramsay Lodge where he lived in the middle room under the three octagonal roofs forming the original dwelling house, seen in old Edinburgh prints. This was later extended to become a block of Ramsay Gardens.

Some Ramsay Lodge members were with him at the foot of the Mound when he was approached by one of the Hot Gospellers who spoke to him thus, "Have you found God?" To which came the reply: "Have you lost him again young man". The only phone in the Lodge was in the basement. Jimmy answered the phone when he happened to be in earshot. He listened patiently then made his response. "I am not my brother's keeper. Good night".

He engendered awe and this was the subject of many stories. At that time religion was more prominent than now and some of the contemporary stories see Jimmy, at least as a Prophet, if not actually in contact with the Almighty.

One story states that Jimmy went to Heaven and was met by Saint Peter who asked Jimmy who he was:

Jimmy: "I am E. B. Jamieson, the famous anatomist."

Saint Peter: "Oh yes, can you prove it."

Saint Peter looked around and saw a woman walking by: "Who is that woman?" he asked.

Jimmy: "That is Eve."

Saint Peter: "Correct, but how did you know?"

Jimmy: "She has no umbilicus, she could not have been born of woman."

Two medical students having completed their dissection for the day and deep in conversation pushed through the double doors of the dissecting room. These doors were half glass but opaque so that unauthorised people were unable to see the ghastly contents of that establishment. To their horror they found the doors had opened against Jimmy himself who had been approaching from the other side. "Good God!" exclaimed one student in consternation. "Yes," said Jimmy, "but strictly incognito."

A terrified student who was standing before his part awaiting the arrival of Jimmy said aloud, "Oh God let me pass". Jimmy approaching silently said, "Boy, I will do my best if you will do the same."

Jimmy was said to have been to see and pay respects at the corpse of Charles, the embalmer, before the funeral. When he came away he said to himself,

"Charles didn't believe in God and he didn't believe in the Devil. There he is all dressed up and there really is nowhere to go".

Jimmy told students whom he felt would not pass, not to waste their money by entering for an examination. One of the boys told not to sit was very religious. He came three or four days later to Jimmy's office and said he had a dream where the Lord advised him to sit anatomy and that he would probably get through. "Please may I sit?" Jimmy replied: "Under the circumstances yes - but before you do please bear in mind your friend is not one of the examiners. I will do the marking".

During his last illness a minister came to see Jimmy and asked, "Have you made your peace with the Lord?" Jimmy answered, "Not as far as I know, I have never had any quarrel with him".

The strength of Jimmy's influence on students was such that it even conflicted with patriotism at times of war, as these anecdotes indicate.

When one young student reached military age he wanted to join the navy. He couldn't do this since he was a medical student unless he failed twice in the same professional examination. Like others he was too afraid of Jamieson to fail in anatomy but he could fail in physiology without giving offence. He did so and was called up and sent to the navy.

A student arrived for his examination on his part of the body resplendent in uniform. Jimmy said, "Boy, why are you dressed like that?" The student proudly replied "I have joined the OTC, sir". Jimmy replied, "Well boy you are also a member of the anatomy training corps. I would suggest you pay more attention to this corpse".

Jimmy was not averse to enjoying a little relaxation at the cinema of which there were three within 600 yards of his department. Two students in the stalls of the Playhouse Theatre were chatting between films the night before an exam in regional anatomy. One said to the other "I wonder what the old B ... is going to ask us tomorrow?", when a head appeared between them and the unmistakable voice said "The old B ... does not know himself yet".

Jimmy returned from a visit to Ferriers, the bookshop opposite the medical school in Teviot Place. The Bedalus resplendent in top hat and top coat, approached him, "Sir, I have one of your students in the lodge completely pickled, that is sir, dead drunk. What shall I do with him?" To which Jimmy replied, "If he does not recover transport the body to the department of anatomy as we are short of bodies".

Perhaps surprisingly Jimmy played golf and many students trudged round the course with him, playing against him as well as carrying his clubs. They recalled the suppers followed by the liqueur which he provided afterwards. These students were amongst those whom Jimmy would invite to a supper of boiled potatoes and herring fried in oatmeal. When the cooking was completed one of the students would be sent to the nearest washroom to heat the plates under the hot tap. On those occasions when Jimmy was entertaining a number of students, he cooked for them large and interesting meals. When the supper was finished small glasses were produced. They were charged from a bottle of liquor hidden in the wardrobe. It appeared to be homemade and was possibly aniseed, a delicious drink. He once said, "When I die and something is written about me in the BMJ you will be able to say that he was also able to cook".

When he was invited for an evening meal he was a charming guest, a great conversationalist and quite different from his austere departmental presence. Two students were sent to bring the great man to dinner at the local hall of residence not far from Teviot Place. As soon as they were seated Jimmy said, "Is it not the custom to say a prayer before the meal?" The student replied, "Oh no sir, just tuck in". Jimmy retorted, "Well boy I think it would be appropriate as a cockroach has died in my soup".

Jimmy was entertained at a hall of residence. The meal ended with nuts. On selecting a walnut, he reached into his pocked, extracted a large folding knife and then deftly split the nut in two. He surveyed his handwork, "Have you ever considered that a walnut resembles a human brain?" He popped the nut into his mouth and at this point an art student fainted.

An American student entertained Jimmy to lunch and as a special treat had obtained a tin of sweetcorn from his parents. Jimmy to student, "What is this?" "Sweetcorn, sir, delicious with melted butter." Jimmy: "They look like deciduous teeth to me".

Jimmy having given so much to others, was also able to ask favours. He used to ask for eggs by sending the empty egg box accompanied by a visiting card back to Dr J's mother. Another student, the son of "a good student" was always asked after a visit, "to request his father to send a bottle of whisky." The whisky always appeared.

He was a mine of information about the affairs, procedures of the management committees and personalities of the university union. He completed more than 40 years of service as a graduate member of the Union Management Committee. His experience and his understanding of students were of constant value to the long succession of office bearers.

When he retired he gave the University of Edinburgh substantial funds for the award of prizes to final year students for knowledge of regional anatomy. These moneys were augmented by royalties on his books which he assigned, in his will, to the university. In his original draft of the regulations for the prizes he stated that the candidates should be members of "what they hope will be their final year".

At the time of his retirement he was content but not lacking in self-confidence. This became more evident as he grew older. In his last years he developed what might be a gerontal narcissism, that is self admiration by the aged for their past. In his last year's Jimmy came to believe he was the best writer of technical English in the world.

THE EDINBURGH – SHETLAND LINK

E. B. Jamieson's Shetland roots remained a strong influence throughout his life.

Male medical students in twos and threes, annually were invited to join Jimmy for a summer visit to Shetland. The students, known in Shetland as the "Un'ken men", were thus privileged to experience and appreciate the two most profound influences which had created the unique character who was Jimmy.

The annual visits to Shetland at the invitation of Jimmy always had the same format, six weeks at his home in Lerwick and a fortnight in a croft at Sandness where his father, Robert Jamieson, had been the country dominie. The routine and programme in Lerwick did not vary for six days of the week but there was a very welcome rest on Sundays.

Jimmy would always say that he wanted a young man to go to Shetland with him to help row the boat. Would the student be interested? Of course he was, especially if he were sitting anatomy that term. Sometimes he was asked again for a second year. If invited for a third year he might receive a letter stating "you may have decided after two summers in Shetland you have exhausted what Shetland has to offer".

The student who had been selected would receive a letter of invitation to Shetland which would read:

My dear ...

I hope you have not got all your vacation period irrevocably fixed up. I need a young man to bear me company and be my galley slave in the Shetland Islands for eight weeks and I hope that you can come and fill that blank.

We will reside in the wilderness half a stone's throw from the sea and if the weather is favourable much of our time is spent on the sea albeit in a rowing boat and for longer distances in a motor boat. The cost to you will be the railway fare and food from wherever you happen to be to Leith or to Aberdeen and the steamer's fare and food from Leith or from Aberdeen to Lerwick. The transport from Lerwick to the wilderness is my charge and I give you board and lodgings. The return ticket from Leith to Lerwick is 69 shillings (£3.45p) and from Aberdeen to Lerwick is 60 shillings (£3). The charge for food on the steamer depends on how many meals you have. Three shillings (15p) for breakfast, four shillings (20p) for midday dinner, half a crown 2/6 (13p) for high tea and two shillings (10p) or 2/6 for supper. I enclose a list of requirements and urge you to try not to lose it. The address is Snarraness, Sandness.

If you can fall in with a map of the Shetland Islands you will find Snarraness jutting out on the southern shore of St Magnus Bay on the west side of the main island.

The ness is a peninsula and the house is on the neck of the peninsula and is literally a stone's throw from the sea. There is no house near it or even within sight. The house is thus in the wilderness.

You must not be fastidious about food, you eat not what you want but what you get. There will however be an abundance of what you get and as much variation as one can expect.

The family is:

1. *James Sinclair, a very large and very strong man.*
2. *Thomasina, his wife, a little woman.*
3. *Magnus - their eldest son, a sailor man at present at home but may go away any day.*
4. *The eldest's son's wife whose name I cannot remember fully. They only married last autumn and I suspect it's Mary.*
5. *Agnes, the eldest daughter, a nurse in Perth and unlikely to be home.*
6. *James, the second son, a sailor man who will probably be at home as he is convalescing from pneumonia.*
7. *The third son, John, another sailor is unlikely to be at home.*
8. *Lorna, the second daughter who is in her teens and will probably be at home.*
9. *Ina, the third daughter of about 15 will be at home.*
10. *Edward, named after me, the fourth son aged 10.*

On your way north send a telegram addressed to me at Snarraness and with these words: "On the way, St Sunniva (the ferryboat), signed J......". Send it from Edinburgh or Leith on Monday in order it may have time to get through to the wilderness. I will arrange for a vehicle for your transport.

Let me set out the diabolics of this sojourn in the north. There are drawbacks. Not enough to deter anyone from coming a second time or even a third time but they should be mentioned.

The weather is very uncertain. Last year we never were thwarted by the weather and took a wicked pleasure in reading about the bad weather in the south but in some summers we have had long spells of westerly winds and westerly winds are cold and boisterous and wet as you Cumberland folk know quite well.

The productive interests of the family are mainly agricultural and pastoral - rather than maritime. In any maritime adventure that we undertake in the motorboat we require to have Mr Sinclair with us as navigator as I know nothing about motors and I don't know where all the sunken rocks are. We have therefore to lend a hand at times in agriculture to expedite these matters and set him free to come with us. When you are aware of any such things that are needed you spring up with alacrity (possibly simulated) and ask what you can do.

You have to labour at an oar or a pair of oars if the wind springs upon us from an adverse direction. You will have exercise on oar, wind or no wind, but I shouldn't call it labour unless there is an adverse wind. If you have learned to pull an oar in an ordinary boat you will probably have to unlearn a lot. If you are quite green then you go through the movements that I prescribe and you pick up the knack in a day or two. (It takes longer if you have movements to unlearn.)

Stormy seas. Anxious mothers. No need for anxiety. The kind of open boat that we have is not shaped like the boats you have seen hitherto and unless mismanaged (and even when mismanaged) will survive any sea. But we hope for little wind.

Last year there were very few fish of any kind, indeed, barely enough for immediate domestic use. But usually we hope to get enough not merely for immediate use but also for a winter supply for James Sinclair's family. We have to salt these fish as soon as they come ashore. We gut those not required for immediate use and lay them in salt and 48 hours afterwards we take them out of the salt and hang them up to dry in the sun, keeping an eye that they do not get wet and put them in the shed if there is rain. The fish we go after are:

1.   inshore ground fish in 10-30 fathoms of water, haddocks, whiting, gurnards and occasionally other kinds - often great numbers of dogfish.

2.   young saithe (or coal-fish) caught round the shores with primitive rods and flies. You take a hand (sometimes a foremost hand) in getting things ready after you have seen what is needed.

The sea is very cold. Too cold for my ageing body and its diminishing chemical activity. But that should not deter you from going in daily. You keep along the shores, for there are sharks outside. Not that I ever did know or hear of anyone coming to harm of a shark in these waters, but they are very ugly looking things.

Requirements:

1.   An ordinary every day suit

2.   An old suit that you don't care what happens to (a pair shorts is a convenient lower part of this suit).

3.   A decent suit.

4.   An everyday pair of boots or shoes.

5.   A decent pair

6.   House slippers

7.   A thick sweater (and two ordinary ones)

8.   Socks or stockings

9.   Collars

10. Handkerchiefs

11. Underclothing

12. Shirts

13. Pyjamas (preferably three suits, as washing in the wilderness is sometimes difficult).

14. A bathing suit.

15. Shaving material

16. Hairbrush

17. Toothbrush

18. Pocket scissors and knife. (Don't forget them: I will not lend mine).

19. Overcoat

20. Money

21. A camera (and films), if you have one, but not specially required.

Yours sincerely,

E. B. Jamieson

E. B. Jamieson's family home in Shetland was at Twageos, Lerwick. This plain but massive house looked over the South Ness beacon and the south entrance to Lerwick harbour and the Bressay Lighthouse. The early history of the house is vague, but its origins date from the 14th or 15th century. Records dated 1641 state that Olaf Magnusson left his father's croft at Brebbisaetr to live in Twageos, which belonged to his dead sister's husband Johannes Vloor. The house had five rooms, " … its own mill, a fifth share in the muckle ane at Heddles, tying for twenty cows and two horses, and a lamb house at Lodberrie". The house was extended in about 1750, the divisions between the old and new could be recognised in the attic and at the junctions between stone and wooden stairs. One worn stone stair tread was used as a lintel. The extended house was originally occupied by the Earl of Morton's retainers.

It stood in front of a spacious garden surrounded by a 10 foot high wall. The house was described by Ronnie Sill, (the pen name of John Harald Johnson, a notable and prolific local writer who published in the *New Shetlander* magazine and other journals). His pen name was derived from his birthplace, close to Ronas Hill, the highest hill in Shetland. He described Twageos as a sprawling farmhouse-cum-ha', with ten rooms on three floors and a large attic or "cocklaft" running the length of the slate covered roof. The house was extended by passages which linked the house to out houses. Though the walls were some six feet thick, the rooms were well lit by ample windows, except on the north side, where the windows were bricked in and the resulting interior cavity was used as a shelved store cupboards. The large front door had a sizeable brass mushroom let into the stone work alongside the jamb, and a brass knob operated an old fashioned pull-bell. The bell couldn't be heard in most of the house, so visitors would enter and knock on room doors until welcomed.

Once inside there was a large hall, divided by a half glassed partition. To the left, or south, was a small passage leading to the parlour, from which led a roofed side passage to a washroom and lavatory. Also to the left of the entrance hall was a large farmhouse kitchen with a low ceiling, flagged floor and a fireplace capable of cooking whole animals, with a gravy pit let into the hearthstone and the residue of a spit. To the north of the kitchen was a passage leading to a servant's bed-sittingroom. From the smaller hall ran a roofed passage way to the back doors, one facing north, the other to the south, each giving access to the flagged area surrounding the house. The passage extended to the dairy, coal and peat stores each with tipping hatches. Further along this passage was a large washroom and bathroom with a large copper boiler and plunge bath, the water for which came by a old type lever pump from a well under the flagged floor. The earlier staircase from the entrance hall was stone, then the wooden addition led up to a landing. A door led through to a corridor, on the north side of which was a large sitting room lit by windows on two sides. Next to this was a guestroom. On the south side was the dining room and large pantry with windows facing the sea. A further flight of stairs ran up to the second floor, with a large bedroom at either end, and two smaller bedrooms between. There was access to the loft from outside the northern bedroom. At the back of the house was a road leading to a paddock and a coach house with a hay store on one side and harness room on the other, all built in stone with slate roofs. To the west of the house was a kitchen garden and to the east the remains of the quarry from which the stone of the house was obtained.

The house was believed to be haunted by a ghost, the "pin-legged fiddler" who would clump about the house. Sometimes his fiddle music could be heard at night, ranging from a slow air to a lively spring. Ronnie Sill lived in the house for four years. His young man's scepticism was shaken by a series of inexplicable sounds and presences. Despite these the house always felt at peace and exuded contentment. Only once did the ghostly presences misbehave, when they appeared to have a fight and a bedroom door was broken, perhaps by a supernatural fist. The house had at some time been fitted with bell pulls or "janglers". The two main bedrooms, the dining and drawing rooms had cranks fitted by the fireplace and connected by wires to a bell board in the kitchen. After these had fallen into disuse, it was said that the ghost was still able to jangle the bells at night. Twageos House was demolished in 1961 and replaced by Coastguard Cottages.

The household at Twageos consisted of four persons. Mrs Jamieson, E. B. Jamieson's mother, his two sisters, Christine and Annie and his nephew Bertie. After the death of the mother, Barbara Jamieson the factor who looked after the farm lived in the house. He was married with children. Neither ownership nor whether there was a partnership was clear.

Jimmy amongst his "ain folk" was a very different person from the Edinburgh anatomist and teacher. At home in Shetland, he varied between being silent and extremely talkative. He was regarded locally as being eccentric, was unconventional and delighted in shocking people whom he did not like. He collected antique silver which was eventually left to his nephew and nieces.

To the local people his annual visit was a highlight of the year. To the student it was a source of life long memories, though he might at times feel like a trespasser. In Lerwick Jimmy was obviously regarded as a very famous man. His fame however related to his strength, manifest by his ability to lift a 10 stone bag of flour off the floor and to put it on to a chair.

When Jimmy and his students arrived in Lerwick he would go to the Saturday market and buy eight lambs. These were killed sequentially during the holiday, providing fresh Shetland lamb. The diet also included fish, potatoes and local cabbage. There was no alcohol consumed in Shetland, it was provided only when they met in his digs.

The students had a number of opportunities to meet members of the Jamieson family. One was the visit for lunch to Jimmy's uncle's house in Lerwick, where they were offered a six course lunch which included herring, roast meat, a pudding and coffee.

As indicated in his letter of invitation, Jimmy's preoccupation during the summer months was to catch fish, salt them and pack them in barrels for the winter. Riding in Bressay Sound was his small rowing boat. This was reached by a five foot dinghy which was carried ashore and launched in a small geo or inlet amongst the rocks. If the sea and weather were at all favourable Jimmy and his students went out every day. Meals were uncertain and the programme each day depended upon the weather. They would come ashore for tea and then fished for saith on the rocks with bamboo wands and hooks until between 10p.m. and 2a.m. The fish were then cleaned, salted and hung. Mackerel fishing was also enjoyed.

Most of the time on the holiday was spent either sailing or rowing. Sometimes they sailed across St Magnus Bay to Hillswick to collect a whole years supply of flour, or to the whaling stations at Collafirth and Ronas Voe. This was a very smelly experience, the stench extending for miles.

A student just back from the sojourn with Jimmy to Lerwick told of how, whilst on the boat, he had been extremely embarrassed to be aware of a niggling and an ultimately urgent wish to pass urine and finally had to explain his predicament and was told to do the obvious. A Shetland boat is sharp at both ends with no comfortable broad and secure thwart on which to stand. Attempting to do what he must do, teetering in this narrow bow or stern, relaxation was impossible and at last, to his immense relief he heard a rewarding tinkle in a calm sea. From behind came that slow and sonorous voice 'Good boy'. Much of the time the boat was caught in the swell, tossed for hours in the waves, always conducive to sea sickness.

Jimmy would wake the student and breakfast was at 9a.m. After breakfast there was a visit to the town harbour for a mackerel for use as bait and then out to the boat. In Lerwick they had a delightful custom, twall which really meant a cup of tea mid-morning. Here Jimmy excelled. At the top of his form he was, as a hostess said, "most lightsome company". Some of his ploys were however a little cranky. The collection of salt for example meant the pushing of a very creaky wheelbarrow right through the town to the west end. All the shopkeepers came to their doors as if to say that "this old fool" had turned up again. Meanwhile his student sweated and took turns at pushing the barrow. Another example of eccentricity was when during the potato famine of the 1914–18 war, Thomasina, the wife of a crofter, had put out a pail of food for the hens. Whilst she was out Jimmy, having walked from Lerwick to Snarraness arrived "clung as a peat" and wolfed all the potatoes from the pail.

If the weather was not suitable for fishing, golf was played on a stony, six hole golf course, at Annsbrae. Golfballs were painted yellow to distinguish them from seagulls feathers with which the course was scattered. Bathing was another activity during the holiday. Jimmy used to swim at a small beach four miles from the main beach. He seldom wore a bathing costume and took only one towel of which the student was allowed the first use.

Whilst in Lerwick the other major activity was hillwalking. The wise old bird knew, as did the student, that they had to get into training for the final target of the 21 miles walk from Lerwick to Snarraness. The mileage alone did not convey an adequate impression of the effort involved. It was mostly over hills and heather. They had to carry on their backs all the luggage required for a fortnight. On these tramps Jimmy was at his best. Though they often slouched along in complete silence for hours at a stretch, at other times he opened up. Every rock and every hill reminded him of an anecdote. Country lore, the flora and fauna of Shetland, seaboats, astrology, astronomy, folklore, history and literature. His favourite period in history was the early Tudor period and the renaissance. His idol was Chaucer.

Even in his battered trilby hat, smoking or chewing a stem of grass he reminded one of a pilgrim. He showed two vulnerabilities on these excursions, thirst and blistered heels. For the first problem, Jimmy would often drink out of a pail or from the spout of a teapot. He always used the flap of an envelope to treat his blistered heels.

He knew all the crofters around Lerwick. He would sit in a croft and chat for hours and when it was nearly dark set off for home (a distance of seven or eight miles. The fortnight spent at Snarraness was the highlight of the Shetland holidays with a glimpse into the crofters' way of life and the introduction into the Sinclair family. Gideon, the patriarch, had been a pupil and lifelong friend of Jimmy's father. Jimmy, the son was a big, powerful man, well over six feet tall with broad shoulders who had been a sailor before settling down. The economy of his croft depended upon sheep. Most of these were pastured during the summer months on one of the many green islands off the coast of the mainland. The croft itself was a two-storey building with a small amount of ground, yielding good crops of oats, hay, potatoes and cabbage. All cultivation was by hand and the hay and oats required to be scythed. Thomasina, Jimmy Sinclair's wife did the housework, cooking and looking after seven children, four boys and three girls remaining after their twins died.

There were visits to an old weaver, Rae Duncan, in Scalloway. He was an intellectual and classical scholar, a self taught expert in Greek and Latin. His daughter, a retired teacher lives in Lerwick.

The young medical students were, as they had been warned, treated as slaves. In Snarraness, each year they built the harbour and a jetty, though each winter the result of their labour was swept out to sea. The friendships formed on these holidays though were usually life long.

Snarraness croft which belonged to the Sinclairs fell into a state of disrepair, but has a new lease of life with a road having been built to a salmon farm. The stone pier on which so many medical students laboured during the summer is crumbling into the sea. The lonely beauty of the site is amplified by the sounds of the sea and the cries of the seabirds, the wild orchids on the hillside and the ever changing pattern of light and water glowing in the summer.

EPILOGUE

E. B. Jamieson always slept badly and had, over the years, taken many and various kinds of sleeping pills. He smoked in bed and died in 1956 after setting fire to his mattress. He was extensively burnt by the time he was found, and was admitted to Ward 7, Royal Infirmary Edinburgh. When Professor Romanes went to see him he looked up from the bed and in keeping with his usual facade said, "Hello, it seems I am burnt." These were possibly his last words.

Jimmy was a bachelor, who never owned any property but lived always amongst students, in lodgings or in student residencies. Thus he knew them and all their problems intimately, possibly his greatest gift to his students. This poem, printed in the student magazine, reflects the awe, gratitude and affection with which he was regarded.

"A Tribute to E. B. J.
Watch him pass with step majestic,
Down cadaver littered room,
On his face one sees depicted,
All this sad world's sorry gloom,
Listen now, his voice majestic,
Tells of nerve in hidden nook,
Then unerring draws it forward,
With his special little hook,
Dear old Jimmy, kindest creature,
Large of heart, of friends the best,
Very many student troubles,
Lurk within that massive breast.
Anon."

There were many obituaries, but perhaps this (by R. M. H.) succinctly encompasses the man "a great anatomist, an erudite teacher, but especially a man of fine character, steadfast faith and simple kindness. He will live long in the thoughts of all who were privileged to know him."

APPENDIX I

SHORTENED version of "Maichie's Ride" by John Cranston (Christina Jamieson).

The story is told of Ion of Mid-Setter in the lonely valley of Vatzdal. In the previous century the valley was a flourishing district. The inhabitants were mostly odal born, (owning and living on land by inherited succession without a feudal lord). At that time much Dutch fishing was carried on round the islands. Ion, who had no surname, was approaching old age but the vigour of his youth was no whit abated. He was the ablest skipper at the haaf, the fleetest of foot on the hills where he kept large flocks of sheep and was skilful in the farming of his land. Men said that he had but one fault: he was quick to take offence and slow to forget it. Ion was well known as a hospitable udaller (as in odaller) but also a contraband trader. The customs were imposed with a slack hand and the feeble coastguard conveniently winked at much he saw.

The Dutch kept a small store at Vatzdal during the summer. Ion took this over and supplied the district for the rest of the year. He had an understanding with the skipper of a small trader who went to Hamburg with fish every autumn and brought back the Tacksman's winter supply. During the winter there were many "comers and goers" at Mid-Setter.

There was then a change in the Custom House when a new customs officer arrived. He was a taiger (tiger) of a man. He scoured the islands, and doubled and trebled the coastguard. Were a keg of gin or tobacco landed, he was on its track like a sleuth hound, and its luckless owner fined with unheard of fines. Smuggling, which had gone on merrily, almost without caution was now conducted with a care and secrecy hitherto unknown. The customs officer even turned his attention to the wrecks, long regarded as the people's right. Men said that he was in league with the Evil One, for no mere man was ever endowed with such relentless activity.

Algroeney and Vatzdal lie so out of the way that the smuggling carried on there escaped this gentleman's vigilance. Soon all the neighbouring coast depended for its contraband upon Algroeney and Vatzdal. The suspicion of the officer was at last drawn to both and he waited for his opportunity to pounce on them. He learnt that the tacksman of Algroeney was the source of the gin and tobacco and that Ion of Mid-Setter supplied the people.

Ion's family life had been somewhat unfortunate. Ion's son had been pressed (forced into service with the Royal Navy) and never heard of again. The shock had caused the death of Ion's wife and had greatly embittered Ion's life. Ion had been gladdened though by the growing graces and beauty of his daughter Inga, now come to womanhood. Inga was small and graceful in form, frank and childlike in her nature with laughter ever ready. She sang sweetly the few ballads that people knew, danced like a fairy, for every maid in Shetland at that time could sing and dance.

It was the crowning accomplishment of a young man that he could play the fiddle and there was music in all homes. In the long winter nights the dalesmen found compensation for all the toils and dangers of the year. It was inevitable that Inga should have many admirers, but she treated all their advances with a gay indifference that wrung the heart of many a wooer. Inga's affections were already bestowed on her cousin Jamie o' Brugarth, with whom she had grown up.

Jamie was very unassuming and his manner to Inga was, so far, brotherly, so few thought of him as her lover. Indeed it was only when he saw the attentions of others to her, that he realised his own feelings. This course of true love might have run smoothly enough but for an unfortunate incident which brought Jamie under Ion's displeasure.

It was an early harvest, and the sheep had to be caaed (driven) in order to take home the lambs before harvesting began. It proved a difficult task, for sheep are very unmanageable in windy weather. The sheep were gathered into one large flock and driven towards the hollow near the top of the hill where the cru (sheepfold) lay. As they neared the cru several people ran forward and ranged themselves at intervals to prevent the sheep from breaking out before reaching the cru door. Jamie was one of these. As the sheep approached him, Inga came round the shoulder of the hill with a few sheep that she had brought from the back and ran past him towards the cru. Her sudden appearance startled him, his foot slipped. The movement startled the foremost sheep, which took out past him over the shoulder of the hill and away down the back. Almost all the flock followed, despite all efforts to stop them.

When Ion came up, his blue eyes glowing in his flushed face like a brimstone upon coal.

"What föl is to wight for this," he asked bitterly; "here's a haill morning lost, after a'wir trouble."

Jamie spoke up "It was me", he said; "an nae man could be mair vexed dan me to be the cause."

"Foo could du play sic a föl's trick?"

"My fit sled on a ston an' I snappered an' gluffed the sheep", said Jamie looking confused.

"Whaur was dy een at du couldna notice dy feet?" inquired Ion, more for the sake of venting his wrath than getting an answer.

Here young Malcolm of Houll, commonly called Lang Maichie, suddenly spoke up. "He was owre trang skoitin' at Inga!"

This showed to Ion that his daughter whom he had always regarded as a child had now become an object of interest to young men. He spoke savagely to Jamie. "Föl!" he said; "to lose our morning's wark to me an' a' Vatzdal, wi' your folly! Never darken my doors again."

"Faider!" cried Inga; "Dinna ba' angry wi' him for nae fault of his. It was me to wight, for I s'ouldna'a run in owre when the sheep were sae near." But Ion turned away and went homewards. That afternoon, Jamie mustered the people and caaed the sheep successfully.

Ion's displeasure was unabated. While he felt he had been hasty, he was still unable to overcome his life-long habit of maintaining a grudge. All through the harvest, on occasions where formerly he would have called Jamie to his assistance, he called Maichie. That young man whose unwieldiness of body and moroseness of disposition rendered him somewhat unpopular, overcame both to a remarkable degree now that he found himself in favour. Love is a powerful quickener, and he did love Inga with all the force of his dull nature.

Hallowmas drew nigh, still the tacksman's trader did not come. Ion occupied the time of waiting by constructing a secret storehouse and enlarging a cave at the voe. It was entered by what appeared to be a "blind hole" on the landward side — an entrance easily concealed by heather. Maichie assisted him in both matters and was raised in Ion's estimation. Ion playfully said to Inga that she might do worse than marry Maichie. Inga took this very hard as she never liked Maichie, did not want him and would not have him.

On Hallow day Ion and most of the dalesmen were on the hill looking after sheep, when in the afternoon they espied the trader, making for Algroeney. Ion returned home to prepare a boat. When he reached home his brother Olla came into the house.

"I fell in with the customs man, and tree sheelds with him, making for St Ninians, he axed me to show dem da wye. So I shew them da wye, an" — with a prodigious wink — " I think it maybe be a while to win dere. I sent my boy to warn da folk at St Ninian's, so dey might keep dem on the mainland a while".

Olla took a crew of the few men from the hill work, and went to meet the trader at Algroeny, get the goods and warn the Tacksman. The boat was to lie off to the westward till after dark and, if all was well, use a light to guide them to the voe.

There was a rant (dance) that night at Thorval's in Uppdal. Thorval was famous for his good ale and his marvellous sea stories. Most of the young people, including Inga, were going to it. Some lads went with a hand barrow to Linga water, beyond the valley to fetch Tammy Cheyne the blind fiddler, without whom no festival was complete.

Tammy had told them to come early otherwise the trows would forestall them. The Trows had a way of fetching Tammy away to celebrate their festivals. But in the dusk the lads came disconsolate, for they could not find Tammy. They met two strangers, however, who had asked the way to Mid-Setter and they had shown them. One went there, the other passed down to the voe. When the lads told this at Uppdal, folk shook their heads and prayed that no harm might befall Mid-Setter.

The rant went on despite Tammy's absence, for there were many amateur fiddlers willing to play for a spell. The barn was cleared for dancing. In the house the elder people peacefully drank their ale, discussed their affairs and spun their yarns, serving the young people when they came in from their dancing.

Ion, warmly wrapped was in the act of taking his lantern to go on his journey along the cliff, when a stranger entered whose appearance caused an instant mental rearrangement of his plans. He divined that the customs officer, having arrived at St Ninians and got his bearings, had sent some of his men to keep guard at Vatzdal.

The stranger was surprised to find Ion at home and suggested he would be the better of company.

Ion laughed, "For all the distance I have to go home to feed my lambs?" The man was not satisfied, "You wrap up well for such a purpose."

"In faith," said Ion, now somewhat nettled; "ye would wrap up too if every joint ached with rheumatism. But ye seem well travelled: will ye not sit down"

The man sat down on the settle. He looked at the long pipes in a double row of leather thongs nailed to the side of the tail press.

"I warrant," he said; "that you have no tobacco or gin to entertain a stranger with." Ion replied cooly; "If it be tobacco or gin ye seek, you have come to the wrong place. Ye will find none in the valley."

"Nor at the voe tonight?" said the man with a peculiar glance.

"If you find any at the voe I shall be glad to see it", answered Ion.

He passed quickly out and went round to the byre. Inga dressed for the rant stood by her favourite cow.

"Inga, I maun pit my trust in dee dis nicht," he said; and told her what she must do. He could not now leave the house without arousing suspicion. She must take the lantern and go to Houll and tell Maichie to take someone with him and go to show the light above the Ha' of Skaga, and when the boat came, within hail, tell them to come in there and stow the goods in that cave.

The Ha' of Skaga is a large cave, considerably above high water, in the cliffs, midway between Vatzdal and St Ninians. It was difficult to access from the sea, as there was no beach below the rocks where a boat could land, so the casks had to be hauled up by ropes, a dangerous task.

"But Maichie is at the rant," said Inga; "he cam' alang for me, but I waited for the lassies."

"Dan du maun fetch 'im frae the rant," said Ion; "de'r nae idder wy 'at we can dö. An' du maun tell Maichie no to lat the boat come near the voe dis nicht, for der a watch in the valley. Dey maun pit her roond to Kirkasting, and nane o' the men maun come to Mid-Setter. Du can bide at the rant till Maichie comes to tell dee when a' is weel, an dan du maun come hame. An' tell Thorval to be careful wi' ony ale or bacha he has, since the customs men are in the dale". Inga put on the cloak which she had on her arm, took the lantern and went tripping lightly up the frozen valley.

Maichie was in no amiable mood that night. He had rushed to escort Inga to the rant, and when he came she flatly refused to go with him. When he came to Thorvals, he went in and comforted himself with a cog of ale. Maichie's misfortune was that he could stand very little drink of any kind. So his ideas were very confused when he left the house, and entering the barn propped himself against the wall to watch the dancing.

Jamie was also at the rant, arrayed in all the glory of white trousers and blue jacket with brass buttons. He sat on the heap of sheaves at the inner end of the barn and took his turn at the fiddle while he awaited the arrival of Inga. His heart leapt to see Inga's fair face and golden head in the doorway. But she beckoned to Maichie and withdrew, and his heart sank in his shoes. He played furiously as he saw Maichie lurch out the doorway. He finished the reel, thrust the fiddle into the hands of the next player and darted past the panting dancers.

Inga told Maichie what she wanted before she perceived that he was in no fit state for the undertaking. She was standing away from him in disgust and perplexity when Jamie's figure appeared outlined in the light of the barn door.

"Oh Jamie, I'm blyde du's come", she said. They moved away from the barn, and she told him her difficulty.

" I'll go", he said taking the lantern with a regretful look at the pretty face that he must leave behind. But she caught his arm. "Oh Jamie! No dysel!"

"An' why no mysel?"

"Da trows, du kens" and she held him fast. Had not the trows taken Tammy Cheyne that very night.

A sudden resolve took Inga; "I'll come, if du'll tak' me."

After she gave her father's message to Thorval, the two of them sped down the dale, up its northward side and away along the cliffs.

Meanwhile the customs officer, having travelled six extra miles thanks to Olla, had descended on St Ninians where his arrival created less surprise than he might have expected. He burst like a whirlpool into the quiet parlour of the little fishcurer at the Booth of St Ninian's, where that meek man sat nursing twins whilst his wife prepared the evening meal. He threatened the fishcurer with all the terrors of the law if he did not instantly man a boat to put him to Algroeney. At last a boat was mustered, and put to sea. In a short time the officer noticed that water was pouring into the boat, and he drew the attention of the nearest man to the fact.

" In faith," said the man, in an assumed surprise; "the nile is oot. What made du o' the nile, Hackie?"

"I believe," said Hackie, with an air of great concern; "I left 'im i' the pocket o' my oilskin. Du has a pair o' gude lang legs: go du an' fetch 'im."

While the officer raged and swore in the stern, the boat had to be put back to the shore, the nile properly fixed and the water scooped out. They put into a tiny creek, set the custom's officer and his companion ashore and showed them a light that they were to make for to reach the tacksman's.

They were pulling rapidly away when they were arrested by a leonine roar.

" Ye scoundrels!" shouted the officer; "You have landed me on a holm! Come back immediately."

Hackie replied; "Sir, an' it had only been dis time last year, ye would a' been staundin' on Algroeney richt anyoch. Bit last winter gales, the sea ture oot yon tongue of laund an' made a holm o'd. An' ye'll hae patience till the ebb; ye can cross on the rocks an' win to the tacksmans still. Gude-nicht, an joy be wi' you."

Meanwhile at Vatzdal, Maichie stood where Inga had left him vaguely trying to make out what she had wanted him to do. Was it not to meet the boat. Well he would meet the boat. He walked up the north side of the valley thinking that the ground was very rough and broken tonight. Presently he became aware that he was accompanied by a pony, which walked close beside him, pushing its mane against his hands. He scrambled on its back and the creature moved resolutely towards the hills on the north. He then tried to dismount, but this the creature resisted.

Machie realised that he was mounted on a nyuggel. This magical creature haunts the lonely hills, lures the wayfarer onto its back and rushes with him into the nearest water — a fate the rider can only escape by a timely appeal to heaven, when the nyuggel disappears in a blue flame.

Maichie struggled to dismount, but this only maddened the creature which galloped furiously along. Maichie tried vainly to recall the words which could save him. Away went his demon steed, up hill, down dale, over moor and bog and moss and peat bank. Machie vented his feelings in loud yells of terror. After a few minutes the thunder of its hoofs told him that they were on the cliff. Below boomed the Atlantic.

"Noo, Lord, deliver me!" groaned Maichie in the depths of his despair. The creature slid from under him, and a great blue flash blazed out over the sea as he came to ground. He lay for a while, incredulous of his escape.

As he lay there, it seemed to him that he heard the strings of a fiddle mingling with the waves below. He moved along the cliff to a place where the cliff sloped somewhat. He was above the famous Ha' of Skaga. Maichie went down the path, familiar from boyhood, and came to the cave's mouth and went in. The old cave was brightly lit up within. Its pillared walls gleamed like marble and many coloured festoons hung from its roof.

Lithe forms leaped and swayed in the mazy dance, accompanying the Trow's Spring played by a fiddler on a high stone slab. The fiddler was none other than blind Tammy Cheyne of Linga water.

"Gude save you!" cried Maichie, "Foo wan ye yonder Tammy?" The music died down in a long squeak, the lights and dancers vanished in a twinkling, and Maichie was stood staring blankly into a dark cave, with patches of phosphorescence gleaming here and there on its walls.

"Wha spak?" cried Tammy's voice out of the darkness and Maichie found his way to his side.

"Foo wan ye here?" he repeated; "Ye, sae sichtless an' fitless 'at folk maun carry you whaurever ye hae to gaing".

"The trows took me doon," said Tammy. "An' noo dus gluffed them awa. Foo am I to win oot o' here, noo?"

Tammy, whose thin form became erect, whose blind eyes flashed and face glowed as he wielded his bow, became a poor, decrepit, querulous creature whenever he laid the fiddle out of his hands. Maichie had to carry him on his back up the perilous cliff, and all the weary way that lay between Skaga and Vatzdal. The fiddler told him to carry him to the rant, since he had spoiled his fun with the trows. At Uppdal his coming was gladly hailed. Maichie lay down among the sheaves and fell asleep.

At Mid-Setter Ion and his unwelcome guest, having adjusted their mutual relations, got on better than might have been supposed. At intervals, the man went out and signalled to his companion at the voe where nothing particular seemed to occur. On occasion, he noticed the merrymaking up the valley hearing the strains of the fiddle and the skirls of the dancers. Ion replied that there was a rant, and the man suggested that they should go to it. Ion consented.

They went to Thorval's who was in the middle of a long sea yarn. When Ion asked for Inga he was told she was in the barn. In the barn, everyone asked, where was Inga? The man was interested in the dancing and offered to dance a hornpipe. Ion walked to the sheaves to see if Inga was there but found to his dismay Maichie lying fast asleep. On arousing Maichie, the only response was that Maichie seemed only to tell him that Inga wanted him to do something that he couldn't make out and had suddenly left him. Ion imagined that Inga had gone to Skaga by herself. The thought of his daughter out on the wild cliffs on her own filled him with anxiety and apprehension.

Inga and Jamie arrived at Skaga shortly after Maichie had left with his burden. They showed a light and were instantly hailed from the sea. Jamie shouted to the men to come nearer inshore, and soon he and Inga were at the foot of the cliff path and told their story.

"Man, Jamie," said Olla, as they proceeded with landing and stowing the goods, "whaar got du sic a famous blue licht?"

"I had nae blue licht" said Jamie puzzled.

"No!" said the astonished Olla; "Man, it cam' oot owre the sea wi' a lowe laek a blue draigon! I said when I saw'd it, Ion said he wad shaw a licht an' faith, he's keepit his wird weel! We wir a braa wye oot, an' we rowed within hail, bit it was a while or we saw ony mair signs o' you".

They feared it had been some coastguard signal and moved with all the greater caution. They were all safe in their homes before midnight.

Ion, chafing and fuming within himself, returned to Mid-Setter still accompanied by the vigilant customs man. He entered the house, and to his exceeding relief, he saw his daughter in the act of hanging up her coat. Her radiant face and her manner indicated that the mission was successfully accomplished.

"I was feared that I had lost dee," said Ion; as he sat down and took her on his knee. "The maid has been walking with her lover", said the man, hitting the mark at random. Inga blushed and looked down. Ion realised that he had not seen Jamie at the rant. He put things together in his mind and arrived at conclusions on which he afterwards acted.

Next morning the coastguard made a vigorous search, but there was nothing suspicious to be found in valley or voe. They went to their superior at St Ninians and reported that they had seen no evidence of smuggling at Vatzdal. That worthy, having waited on the holm until low water reached the tacksman's house and found no contraband in trader or store or neighbourhood. He returned to the mainland, deeply chagrined and mortified, for he had never been so effectually foiled before.

At Vatzdal, blind Tammy soon let out his own and Maichie's adventures which excited great mirth. The boatmen maintained that for a signal light there was nothing to beat an exploding nyuggel.

"Send Maichie wi' a nyuggel" when a light was wanted passed almost into a proverb.

"So Jamie guid wi dee to Skaga", said Ion to Inga at the first opportunity.

"O fader," said Inga with swimming eyes, "I dinna ken what I would 'a dune withoot Jamie."

"I daursay no", said Ion again

He met the young man soon after. A few weeks afterwards, Jamie appeared at Mid-Setter, with his spöring-bottle, his manner invested with a new kind of bashful importance. He had come to ask for Inga. This was readily given, but not the farm as yet, as Ion still had not given up hope for his son's return.

So there was held at Mid-Setter the merriest wedding that ever gladdened the valley of Vatzdal.

APPENDIX II

The Jamieson Family Tree

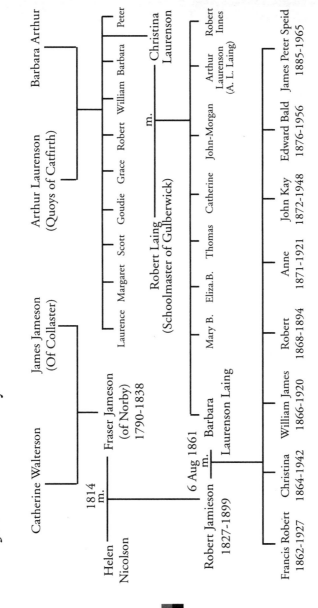

Acknowledgements are made to the family tree drawn by J. P. S. Jamieson with details added to and confirmed by Mrs Thelma Watt, Shetland Family History Group.

GLOSSARY
OF SHETLAND WORDS

aamos	a gift
ain	own
anyoch	enough
ax	to ask
bacha	tobacco
bain	thick leather used for the soles of shoes
berg	a prominent rock
bide	dwell, stay
bit	only
blaand	sour whey
blue litt	indigo dye
blyde	glad
braa	grand , splendid
bridder	brother
caa	a drive of sheep or whales
cast	(n) skillful manner of working
	(v) to dig peats.
clock	a beetle ; witchy clock - witches beetle.
clew	a tangle
'clung as a peat'	hungry
corbie	raven (corvus corax)
craigs	rocks along the foreshore; rockfishing
craigsaet	a cup-shaped hole in a rock; a craig suitable for craig fishing
craigstane	see craigs
crö	sheepfold
crook	a hook from which pots were hung over the open fire; a sheep-mark involving a semi-circular piece taken out of one side of the, ear , "a crook oot ahint"
da	the
dan	then, at that time
dat	that
der	their
der	contraction of dey wir, there is/are
dere	there
du	you, (familiar)
dy	your
dysel	yourself

een	eyes
ess	ash, ashes
faat	injury, harm
fey	bewitched, halfwitted
fitless	unsteady
flae	to cut turves off the surface of peat-bank.prior to casting
flee	fishing fly
föl	fool
foo	how
frae	from
gifgaf	give and take.
girse	a grass
gizzen	to dry up
gluff	(n) a fright
	(v) to frighten
gös	goose
guddick	a riddle; phrase. To lay up guddicks is to ask a series of riddles.
Gude	God
ha'	house
Haa,Ha'	Laird's house
haaf	the deep sea beyond coastal waters
Hallowmass	hallowe'en
helyer	a sea cave into which the tide flows
holm	islet
howdie	a midwife
kale	a leaf vegetable
ken	to know
kishie	straw basket or creel
kist	chest, trunk, coffin
kistin	the laying of a dead body into its coffin
knock-soe	mashed limpets, made by pounding limpets in a hole in a rock (a Craigsaet).
laft	the upper story of a two story house
lowe	(n) flame, blaze
	(v) to burn brightly
lug	human ear
maun	must
moose	a mouse
muckle	big
nae	no
nane	none
nicht	night
nile	the plug in the nile-hol of a boat
nile-hol	a small hole in the bottom of a boat for draining out the bilge water.

Norn	a variant of the Old Norse language, which survived as the native tongue of Orkney and Shetland until the 17th Century.
Nyuggel	a legendary waterhorse of Shetland folklore
odal-born	owning and living on land by inherited succession, without a feudal lord
ony	any
ös	use
oot	out
owre	over
pirm	a bobbin , a reel of cotton
pör	(n) physically incapable (adj) poor
Ranselman	a Constable appointed under the old Country Acts with authority to search for stolen goods and to apprehend the thief. He was also empowered to keep order in his local Parish. He was active in the 18th and first half of the 19th centuries.
rant	to behave boisterously; a dance. The Shetland Rant, prolonged Christmas and New Year celebrations in Shetland.
reel	a commotion.
reestit	smoke dried
sair	be sufficient
shap	to chop, to mash, as with potatoes.
sheeld	fellow
shöl	to empty out with a shovel.
sic	such
sicktless	blind
sixern	a six oared boat.
Skeo	a hut for storing and wind-drying fish or meat. No longer in use but may be applied critically to a poorly built house
skoit	to look with a purpose
skrotti	a lichen
smora	clover (Trifolium repens)
snapper	to stumble
sooans	a dish, eaten like porridge, made from the husks of corn or oatmeal, steeped in water, fermented and strained leaving a mealy substance (sooans) and liquid (swats). The sooans are boiled before eating
spör	to ask for, enquire, propose marriage
spöring bottle	a bottle of whiskey brought by a young man to the father of his intended bride.
stae	a shawl
stane	a stone
ston	a stone

strae	straw
Strupalty	the Devil.
swats	the liquid in which oatmeal has been steped in making sooans
taiger	a tiger
tak	to take
Tammasmass	St Thomas's day, 21st December traditionally regarded as a day of rest.
trang	very busy
tree	three
trooker	a disreputable woman
trow	a mischievous fairy
tushkar	a spade with a feathered blade for cutting peats
twa	two ; a few
twall	a cup of tea mid morning
twartree	two or three
voe	an inlet into the land, generally long and narrow
weel	well
win	to go, to get (past tense) wan (past participle) wun
wye	way

REFERENCES

1. *Hjaltland Miscellany*, Vol.2, ed. Jamieson, Christina and Reid Tait, Lerwick, 1937.

2. Jamieson, Christina, various articles written under the pen name of John Cranston,
    "The Social life in Shetland"
    "Women, the Spinners and Dyers of Shetland"
    "Child Life"
    "Arts and Crafts in Shetland"
    "A Shetland Whale Hunt"
    "The Eela"
    "Peat Leading in Shetland"
    "Haaf Men of old Shetland"
Introductory essays,
    "The business of the Old Kirk Session" — referring to the whole series of Kirk Session Records.
    "Shetland Education in the 18th Century" for the education records published by E. S. Reid Tait, 1937.

3. Lowther Clarke, *The History of the SPCK*. London, SPCK, 1959.

4. Spence, John, *Shetland Folklore*. Johnson and Greig, Lerwick, 1899.

5. Norie, John William, *A Complete Set of Nautical Tables*, originally published 1803 for the author and for William Heather at the Navigation Warehouse, Leadenhall Street, London.